47th Edition

Ready or Not

Your Retirement Planning Guide

Revised by
Staff members of the
International Foundation of Employee Benefit Plans

Based on content written by
Elizabeth M. McFadden

International Foundation *if*®
OF EMPLOYEE BENEFIT PLANS

Education | Research | Leadership

Principal Contributor: Jenny Lucey, CEBS
Editor: Robbie Hartman, CEBS

Copies of this book may be obtained from:
Publications Department
International Foundation of Employee Benefit Plans
18700 West Bluemound Road
Brookfield, WI 53045
(888) 334-3327, option 4
bookstore@ifebp.org
Payment must accompany order. Call for price information or see www.ifebp.org/bookstore.

Published in 2020 by the International Foundation of Employee Benefit Plans, Inc.
© 2020 International Foundation of Employee Benefit Plans, Inc.
ISBN 978-0-89154-816-4
Printed in the United States of America

PU196187

9M-1219

Table of Contents

Introduction

"A goal without a plan is just a wish."

—Antoine de Saint-Exupéry

The Time of Your Life

Today more than ever before, aging is an opportunity, not a problem. Rather than growing old in retirement, the focus is on living young in retirement. When you retire, you may have the opportunity to pursue quality time with family and friends, hobbies, volunteering and education. You may need to or want to work for the income, routine, satisfaction and social connections that a job provides. And hopefully you have the energy and resources to achieve personal goals.

Have you prepared yourself for this new opportunity? This book is designed to help you look clearly and positively at the changes and decisions of retirement. From where to live to managing stress, caregiving or traveling, we clearly and directly address the financial, physical and emotional concerns you may have about retirement.

An Aging Nation

The first thing to know about aging in America is that "everybody's doing it." Between now and 2030, those over age 65 will become a dominant segment of America's population. In 1900, average life expectancy was 50 years. The concept of 65 as a retirement age appeared in the 1930s, when the average American could not expect to live that long. In comparison, today about one out of every three 65-year-olds will live past age 90, and about one out of seven will live past age 95, according to the Social Security Administration. People are living longer, healthier, more active lives. But the increased life span also comes with the concern of outliving your money.

Ready or Not

Ready or Not is designed to help you consider the full spectrum of retirement planning considerations. Some things are more fun to think about than others. If you come across a topic that you have not yet considered and want further details, each chapter provides resources for more information.

Experts and professionals have contributed specific, detailed information in clear, concise language that will answer your questions about retirement.

Checklists and worksheets make it easy to pinpoint areas of major concern or interest. *Ready or Not* can be your guide to making the most of what can be the best years of your life.

When Will You Retire?

Because many workers today maintain youthful vigor and mental sharpness, they have greater freedom in selecting a retirement age. Some people want to retire before age 65, and others want to work beyond age 70 or as long as possible. This book will help you think about factors such as when to claim Social Security, feeling ready to retire, paying for medical expenses and many more issues that may influence your decision on when to retire.

You may be reading this book and thinking, "I will not be retiring for a long time." But that may not be so. More and more of us are facing retirement sooner than anticipated because of health conditions or caregiving demands. Also, much of the information covered in *Ready or Not* is relevant at all ages and stages of work. And, as the title suggests, it is intended to make you aware of the need to start planning for your future today.

Who Are You Planning With?

Ready or Not suggests a variety of topics to discuss with the important people in your life. If you have a family, it's especially important to discuss and plan the impact of retirement on your spouse and children—and perhaps your parents. People who are single should talk with close relatives and friends. For everyone, retirement should be about retiring to something, not retiring from something. Financial planning is easier if it's shared.

Many couples enter retirement without understanding each other's retirement dreams. Nor do they discuss openly what adjustments they expect to make. This is the time for couples to see if they share the same retirement ideas and to take time for a reality check to plan a happy retirement. The age at which each of you will retire determines how much money you'll need.

Where Are You in the Planning Process?

Surprises are fun for parties but, in daily life, surprises are usually not good news. Early planning is ideal but, if that was not a reality for you, it is OK. Start now. The first step to enjoying retirement is self-awareness. Some questions to guide your personal inventory include:

- How is my mental and physical health?
- Am I financially ready for retirement? A realistic look at your financial situation is crucial. Discuss financial goals openly with the important people in your life. What expenses do I expect in retirement for basic needs and nonessentials? How will my savings and investments turn into my retirement paycheck?
- What will I do with my time in retirement?
- What motivates me? What makes me feel useful?
- How strong are my social connections outside of work?
- What life transitions might I face in retirement?

It is OK if you are unsure of some answers. The goal is to become aware of what to plan for and make sure it rings true to your personal circumstances. This process of comprehensively looking at your lifestyle happens gradually and may change over time.

What Does Successful Retirement Mean to You?

Planning ahead by looking clearly and honestly at the future will give you the confidence to handle what life brings. Planning ahead includes planning to be flexible. Optimism and acceptance of change are linked to longevity. What success looks like is subject to change as you age. You may need to flex your goals, skills, spending and time. *Ready or Not* is designed to help you feel empowered to set yourself up for success, however you define it.

Aging

Did You Know

- More than 47.8 million people age 65 years or older live in the United States, constituting 15% of the population.

- We achieve peak muscle mass by our early 40s. By simply engaging in activities like walking or gardening, you can help slow down the loss. Exercise has benefits at any age. But be sure to check with your doctor before starting any exercise activity.

- Eighty percent of people over 65 have at least one chronic health problem that could limit their activities. Two factors that are important to extended health and happiness are (1) an understanding of one's self (physically, mentally and socially) and (2) good medical care in early and later life.

- The ability to learn new skills and acquire new information remains relatively unchanged from age 20 through age 60. Intellectual powers do not decline as rapidly as people think. The proverb was wrong: You can teach an old dog new tricks!

- Comprehension and vocabulary abilities hold strong through age 60. Physical dexterity and

reaction to stimuli reach a peak at age 18, with a slow decline after age 40. The ability to learn, though, is relatively unaffected by age.

- Of all married couples over age 65, the percentage living in their own households is 78%.

- Fifty-five percent of unmarried individuals over 65 live on their own.

- The average couple has 35 to 40 years of partial leisure after their children are grown.

- An estimated 80% to 120% of preretirement income is necessary to enable the retired person to maintain his or her previous level of spending and living. Some expenses, including work-related expenses (eating out, clothes, transportation) and taxes, will decrease. Other expenses such as health care, travel and leisure activities, energy expenses and costs incurred helping parents or children may increase. And inflation will affect buying power. The Employee Benefit Research Institute (EBRI) found that in the first five years of retirement, more than 50% of retirees spent the same as or more than they did while working.

Where Do I Stand?

This list is designed to increase your awareness of retirement planning considerations.

Yes No

○ ○ I know approximately what my Social Security and pension income will be in retirement.

○ ○ I have a financial savings plan for retirement and am out of debt.

○ ○ I know the approximate future income from my investments, e.g., IRAs and savings.

○ ○ I have completed a net worth statement.

○ ○ I have analyzed my cash flow—monthly and yearly.

○ ○ If married, I have discussed finances with my spouse.

○ ○ I have an up-to-date will, a power of attorney and a health care proxy.

○ ○ I have my important papers, including my will, where my family can find them. If married, I have reviewed the papers with my spouse.

○ ○ I practice good health habits like walking daily, not smoking and drinking in moderation.

○ ○ I have a medical examination each year.

○ ○ I've checked my health insurance coverage, both current coverage and coverage during retirement.

○ ○ I check my home for safety and maintenance.

○ ○ I've discussed retirement plans—e.g., where to live, what to do with time— with the important people in my life.

○ ○ I maintain relationships with friends and am involved in at least one social activity such as volunteer work, civic or religious activities, etc.

○ ○ I am enrolled in an educational or skill-advancement course that interests me and will open doors for new experiences in retirement.

○ ○ I am aware that many people are still in the workforce in their 60s and am prepared for a longer work life.

○ ○ I know that life often does not go as planned and have built a financial safety net. I will take into account losing a job, inflation, health care, caregiving and a long life.

○ ○ I am planning my retirement with the knowledge that life expectancy charts show an average of ages. I may live longer. Some people live close to 100.

Financial Planning

"Retirement is like a long vacation in Las Vegas. The goal is to enjoy it to the fullest, but not so fully that you run out of money."

—Jonathan Clements

Your Financial Future

Where do you stand? Are you a young person just entering the business world? At the midpoint of your career? Rapidly approaching retirement?

Whatever your situation, it makes good sense to regularly and thoroughly review your financial status and do some sound and intensive planning for the future. This chapter will help you do just that. A rich, rewarding life doesn't happen by accident. Whatever your goals are for personal or family life, career, finances, etc., the best means of achieving them is through planning. And it is never too late to start planning.

Planning Is Vital

Ask yourself what you want. List your most important goals first. Decide how many years you have to meet each specific goal because when you save or invest, you'll need to find an option that fits your time frame.

A careless approach to family finances makes life more difficult. Without planning, family funds may be spent in wasteful ways, without much left for savings and investments. Unnecessary borrowing also can burden people with expensive interest.

There are always major financial needs looming that may further complicate matters: a new furnace, car or house; children and their often costly needs, particularly college educations; and, finally, retirement, which often means at least 15 to 20 years of living without a full monthly paycheck.

Note: As you are planning your financial future, be aware that there may be changes in laws that will affect your assets. Keep informed, and consider checking with a financial planner or tax advisor.

Inflation's Impact

Inflation is a sneaky yet important factor. We know it is happening, but we don't give sufficient attention to the effect it has on every dollar we earn and save. In the 20-year period from 1999 to 2019, according to the Consumer Price Index, the value of your dollar decreased 54%. Let's say you withdraw $1,000 a month for expenses. After ten years of 4% inflation, your monthly withdrawal of $1,000 would have the buying power of $675.56—a 34% plunge.

Inflation reduces the value of your dollar, making it a threat to your retirement lifestyle. You will have to consider this in your financial planning, particularly if you are living on a fixed income.

Four Keys to Planning

A sound financial plan is crucial to ensure comfortable living and as a safeguard against personal needs, crises and inflation.

This chapter outlines how to develop a plan, focusing on four important elements:

- Computing your net worth
- Evaluating your cash flow and debt management
- Developing a practical and effective budget
- Setting up a consistent, diversified and balanced investment plan to ensure an adequate level of future income.

Note: At the end of this chapter, you will find worksheets for computing your net worth and cash flow.

The First Step

The first step is to start developing a personal financial plan. It is important to determine your current financial status so that you can develop a long-range plan to help achieve your financial goals. This primarily involves computing your net worth with the worksheet on page 34. Your net worth is simply the difference between your assets (what you own) and your liabilities (what you owe).

To start, gather all financial papers and reports that provide information on your assets and liabilities. These will include items such as savings records, bank statements, checkbooks, statements for certificates of deposit (CDs), stocks, bonds, mutual funds, etc., and similar reports on your residence, vehicles, mortgages, loans, etc.

You should have all of these records stored in one place and organized for easy reference. If they are not so organized, this is an opportunity to correct the situation for future reference.

To locate the market value of some of the items listed on the Net Worth Worksheet, tax records can be helpful, and an online search of reputable websites can give you a good idea of the value of such assets as your home, car(s), tools and equipment, etc.

Your Net Worth

This computation tells you whether or not your assets (cash, bank accounts, stock, etc.) exceed your liabilities (mortgage, credit cards, etc.)—and by how much. If your assets are larger than your liabilities, you have a positive net worth. If your liabilities are larger than your assets, you have a negative net worth.

With this information, you can evaluate your current financial condition in a systematic way. Review the figures, asking the questions:

- Do I have a major financial problem, with my assets barely exceeding my liabilities?
- Is my life insurance adequate for my family's needs?
- Do I have sufficient money set aside in liquid funds for our current needs and potential emergencies?
- Are my investments properly planned and diversified?
- Am I paying off my highest interest rate debt first?

Richer . . . or Poorer?

You'll want to update your net worth statement every year so that you can see how your net worth is growing. Don't be discouraged if you have a negative net worth—Following a financial plan will help you turn it into a positive net worth. In evaluating this growth, look for two things:

- Steady growth from year to year
- A growth rate that exceeds the inflation rate by a substantial amount.

Shame is a common emotion people have when they become aware of an imbalance between their spending and saving. Shame makes it harder for people to ask for help and take action. You are not alone. It is what it is. This chapter will help you focus on ways you can feel empowered to take actions like automating savings, thinking differently about your spending choices and visualizing your future self.

If the growth rate is low or uneven, compare the current year's net worth computation alongside last year's and determine any areas of weakness. How are your investments growing in value? Are your debts being reduced?

By knowing where you stand financially, you will be more mindful of your financial activities, better prepared to make financial decisions and more likely to achieve your financial goals.

Second Step: Your Cash Flow

If a look at your net worth (and the trend in its growth—or decline) suggests something needs to be done to improve your financial status, the best way to get a precise understanding of the problem is to compare your *expenses* with your *income* in a specific way. The worksheet for computing your cash flow (page 33) will help you do this.

Determining your cash flow shows you whether or not your expenses exceed your income—or vice versa. If expenses exceed income and you are losing ground financially, you need to take corrective action. If, on the other hand, expenses and income balance out, then the question is whether or not sufficient funds are being set aside for savings and investments.

The most difficult information to get involves cash purchases. Either estimate these figures from personal experience or keep a journal on these items for several weeks to establish a spending pattern.

Don't expect to achieve perfect accuracy with this analysis. Even an imperfect job will give you a strong starting point for understanding and improving your financial status.

Determining Cash Flow

This takes some doing, so give yourself adequate time to do the job right.

Use the living expenses listing on the form as your initial guide, taking one category at a time to find the needed information. Much of this information can be obtained from your checking account, your credit card and online payment statements, or your tax records.

18% of workers age 50-plus said their household does not have any debt.

For those who do, the three most common types of debt were:

 Credit cards

 Mortgages

Car loans.

If you have a family, you will probably find that many of the expense-reduction measures you decide upon will not penalize any one individual. However, if your financial condition is seriously out of balance, more drastic measures must be taken. The decisions reached should be agreed upon by both partners, with the rest of the family also having input.

What Next? Control Spending

If you have just completed the Cash Flow Worksheet, you know whether your expenses exceed your income. If you are spending all your income and never have money to save or invest, start by cutting back on expenses.

Consider if something is a need or a want. Do this conscientiously, and use the extra money to further beef up your savings and investments.

Cutting back on expenses is not as difficult as you might think. Most of us have let items once considered luxuries become necessities.

This becomes apparent if we closely study the different elements of our expenses. Save $20 here, $10 there, and savings can quickly add up to $150 to $250 a month, which is a tidy sum that can help in the balancing process.

Even if your income exceeds expenses, it's still a good idea to evaluate and control spending practices.

Examine Your Spending

Look at your listing of expenses. The list covers practically all the ways you spend your hard-earned income. So take each category and study it carefully.

Take plenty of time, and thoroughly evaluate the expenditures one item at a time. Be sure to ask yourself the right questions:

- Am I paying myself first by saving and investing?
- Is this product or service really essential?
- Is there a less expensive version of the item?
- Are we using more of the product or service than we really need?
- Are we buying at a good, competitive price?
- Can I take care of any maintenance services myself?
- Would I be able to save by refinancing debt?
- Can I save on my mortgage by paying ahead? **(See Mortgage Math below.)**
- Do my insurance policies provide the protection I want?

MORTGAGE MATH

Here is an example of the difference between a monthly payment and a monthly payment with an additional monthly payment toward the principal on a 30-year $200,000 mortgage at 4% interest.

	Payment	Extra Payment*
Monthly	$954	$200
Annually	$11,448	$13,848
Total interest paid until maturity	$143,739	$100,432
Years to maturity	30 years	21 years, 10 months

*It must be noted on the check or online that the additional payment is toward the principal. Check to make sure you can prepay your mortgage without penalty.

Spending Patterns

It is very helpful to compare the percentage of income you spend on each category with a break-down of the following budget for the average retired couple (source: Bureau of Labor Statistics).

Housing	33%
Transportation	15%
Food	13%
Medical care	13%
Entertainment and education	7%
Insurance/pension	6%
Charity	5%
Clothing	2%
Personal care	1%
Other	5%

If your percentages vary widely from the table above, this is another clue to the categories in which you may be overspending.

Your Expense Reduction Action Plan

Follow your review with a written action plan. As you study each category, decide what, if any, reduction plan you want to implement, and note it under the appropriate heading in the action plan.

You probably can't implement all reductions at once. Instead, prioritize the reductions, putting the most significant first in line. Set a deadline for completion of each one. This puts some pressure on you to make your plan work.

Start taking the actions called for, handling one item at a time. As you complete each action, cross it off your list. Envisioning what your ideal retirement looks like can help you stay motivated to spend less and save more.

Note: If you take every category in your listing of expenses and go through them in this way, you can be sure of this: Unless you are the neighborhood's greatest efficiency expert, you will find a lot of savings possibilities that will help you find your balancing act.

Debt Management

Deciding how to balance debt repayment and savings is a challenging, personal choice. Important factors include how close you are to retirement, how likely you are to face an emergency and interest rates. There are pros and cons of forgoing saving for retirement and emergencies in order to pay down debt. An example of a drawback is missing out on matching contributions to retirement accounts. Or if you don't have savings to cover an emergency, you might need to use a high-interest credit card.

Start by knowing where you stand. Make a list of all the creditors you owe by getting a free copy from each of the three major credit reporting bureaus—Equifax, Experian and TransUnion—by visiting **www.AnnualCreditReport.com.**

List every creditor with an open account, and either obtain your statements or call them to find your current balance, payment due date, minimum payment and interest rate. List all of these debts on a spreadsheet or single piece of paper so you'll have all the information together at a glance. If you don't have money to make all your payments, contact your creditors about what options you may have.

Credit Card Debt

No investment strategy pays off as well as, or with less risk than, eliminating high-interest debt. Most credit cards charge high interest rates—as much as 18% or more—if you don't pay off your balance in full each month. If you owe money on your credit cards, the wisest thing you can do is pay off the balance in full as quickly as possible. Virtually no investment will give you returns to match an 18% interest rate on your credit card. That's why you're better off eliminating all credit card debt before investing. Once you've paid off your credit cards, you can budget your money differently and begin to save and invest.

Here are some tips for eliminating credit card debt:

- If you have unpaid balances on several credit cards, there are two main ways to tackle the debt.

  – Avalanche method: Some people are motivated by paying less interest. Make a list of debts from highest to lowest interest rate. Pay off the highest interest balance first, keeping up with minimum payments on the others at the same time.
  – Snowball method: Some people need to see quick progress to stay motivated. Make a list of debts from smallest to largest. Pay off the smallest balance first, keeping up with minimum payments on the others at the same time.

- Don't use a credit card unless you know you'll have the money to pay the bill when it arrives. Some people like to put day-to-day expenses on a credit card to get rewards from the credit card company. If you do so, be sure to pay off the statement balance in full every month.

- It's easy to forget how much you've charged on your credit card. Every time you use a credit card, track how much you have spent and figure out how much you'll have to pay that month. If you know you won't be able to pay your balance in full, try to figure out how much you can pay each month and how long it'll take to pay the balance in full. Budgeting apps can help with this. **(See page 11.)**

DEALING WITH DEBT

Federal Trade Commission Consumer Information: www.consumer.ftc.gov/topics /dealing-debt

The nonprofit **GreenPath, Inc.,** with offices nationwide, offers free or low-cost budget planning and assistance in working out financial difficulties. Call (800) 550-1961, or visit www.greenpath.com.

Student Loan Debt

Managing student loan debt will affect your cash flow.

Student loan debt is particularly challenging for women. Women hold nearly two-thirds of the outstanding debt. Data from the American Association of University Women shows that women graduate from college with higher loan amounts than men. Women with student debt are more likely than men to not graduate from college due to lack of quality affordable child care. The gender pay gap has a negative impact on student loan debt as well. Women take longer than men to repay loans, therefore paying more interest over the life of the loan.

AARP reports that student loan debt is soaring among older adults and is endangering retirements. Americans age 50 and over account for 20% of the $1.5 trillion student loan debt.

The Consumer Financial Protection Bureau (CFPB) says the number of older consumers with student loan debt has quadrupled over the last decade, and the average amount they owe has also dramatically increased. The CFPB says this makes people age 60 and older the fastest growing age segment of the student loan market.

Some people carry their own balances from starting a second career.

Some people sign or cosign for children's and grandchildren's student loans; you must understand the risk you are taking. Think carefully about paying for college for a relative. What is the return on investment for the student's expected college degree? What is the total cost of the college? How does that compare with their ability to repay the loans? Take the emotion out of the situation, and think before you sign for a child or grandchild.

If you don't have money to make the monthly payments, contact your loan servicer about your options to avoid default. The CFPB says nearly 40% of student loan borrowers 65 and older are in default. If you default on federal loans, the federal government can garnish your Social Security benefit checks. As much as 15% of Social Security payments can be withheld to repay student loan debt, but Social Security monthly checks cannot be reduced to below $750 per month, an amount that is not adjusted for inflation each year. **For more information, go to www.consumerfinance.gov /consumer-tools/student-loans.**

Loaning Money to Family

Relatives who loan money should draw up a simple document describing the terms of the loan, including interest rate and schedule for repayment. Before considering giving a loan, be sure that it will not destroy a relationship if it is not repaid. Be sure that you can afford not to be repaid and that the loan will not jeopardize your retirement. In setting the interest rate, be aware that you must pay tax on any interest earned. Guarantee a relative's credit only if you are prepared for the risks. Do not co-sign unless you can afford the payments yourself.

Your Credit Score

Lenders use your credit scores to help them decide how likely you are to repay a loan or credit card balance on time. The higher your scores, the more likely you are to be approved for loans and qualify for lower interest rates, which will save you money. Certain behaviors can gradually increase your credit scores:
- Continuously pay your bills and credit cards on time.
- Apply for and open credit accounts only as needed.
- Check your credit reports at all three credit reporting bureaus (Equifax, Experian and TransUnion) for any errors.

Third Step: Set Up a Budget

If you have been developing a financial plan along the suggested lines, you have examined your spending habits, projected adjustments in that spending pattern and set up, in effect, a yearly spending budget by category.

BUDGETING APPS

Here's a short list of a few budgeting apps to consider. You may need to try more than one to see what works for you.

- Goodbudget
- Mint
- Pocket Guard
- You Need a Budget (YNAB)

Put this planned spending pattern in a budget form that you can use to control your spending, manage your debt and achieve your financial goals.

Why a Budget?

Besides the obvious advantages of eliminating waste and controlling expenditures, there are a number of additional advantages to living by a budget.

- Having a budget makes the task of achieving financial security much easier. It is a road map to help you reach your objectives with fewer delays and wrong turns.
- You know where you stand financially from month to month.
- It helps generate money for that all-important investment program that will enable you to meet major expenses down the line (home, children, college, retirement).

Tips to Get You Started

Many people give up on budgets because they don't use good judgment in setting them up in the first place. To avoid this, consider the following suggestions outlined by many financial planners.

- If married, continue to approach your working budget as a family project with both partners—

and children, too—having input. If decisions are not made on a truly mutual and fair basis, family members just won't work to make the project succeed.

- Keep the budget format—and the necessary administration of the program—as simple as possible. As you go along, you may find ways to eliminate unnecessary details or recordkeeping. Don't forget your primary objective and the importance of knowing where you stand. Accept the first few months as a trial-and-error period. Carefully evaluate what you are doing. Make necessary adjustments in allocations and in the way you keep records.

Keeping Budget Records

Standard budget books, as well as budget software packages, are widely available online and in stores. Many of them are well-designed, and instructions for their use are spelled out in detail. If you're using pen and paper, you can use the format from the Cash Flow Worksheet in this section to set up your budget record. Search online for free budget spreadsheet templates. Select the one that suits your style.

One feature to look for in particular is a thorough breakdown and listing of various types of expenditures. You need such a listing so that you can track where your money is going in detail.

Track Your Spending

Whichever budget method you select, the format of the monthly record will be reasonably self-explanatory. Here are a few suggestions that may further simplify the process for you.

- Look at all the accounts that make up your budget (checking, savings, credit card, payment apps, digital wallet). Transfer the appropriate information to your budget record at least once a month if your budget method doesn't automatically sync with your accounts.
- Set up a plan to keep track of cash purchases. One way is to keep receipts for all cash

purchases, checking to be sure they clearly show the items purchased and the prices paid.

- Where no receipt is provided, keep a listing in a notebook you carry for that purpose. With these notes, it is easy to update your budget record.
- Another control on small-item purchases is using a purchase order approach. Establish a limit on an item, such as meals out, and limit spending to that level. The amount spent should be the amount budgeted—or less.

Budgeting as a Couple

It's relatively common for adults who combine finances with a partner or spouse to commit financial deceptions against a loved one. The National Endowment for Financial Education has studied financial infidelity and reported that 75% of people surveyed said financial secrets have affected their relationships in some way. Actions that may seem harmless, perhaps hiding an impulse purchase or keeping a little cash on the side, can escalate to offensive actions like hiding an account or lying about income or debt. Keeping debt secret can cause arguments, erosion of trust and, in some cases, even lead to breakup or divorce, not because of the debt but due to the secrecy. Fear, embarrassment and the desire for privacy were reasons that coupled people gave for keeping financial secrets. To maintain trust with your partner, be honest and create a plan together to improve the situation. Making financial decisions as a couple starts with agreeing on goals and a budgeting system.

Keeping your budget program working is the last and most important step in the budgeting process. This starts with a clear assignment of responsibilities.

- Who is going to be responsible for keeping the budget records? This must be specified so that the job gets done regularly.
- How is responsibility for controlling different categories of spending to be divided between household partners? Cash purchases of food, entertainment, personal care and miscellaneous

items can be particularly problematic. You should look at this matter together, using recent experience as your guide, and make a list of the specific items for which each will be responsible.

- Where do you keep the budget funds so they are safe yet readily available? Some people choose a joint checking account; others choose a savings account and a checking account. Separate checking accounts are a third way. With this system, an appropriate allocation of monthly income is made to each account to cover assigned expenditures. Each spouse draws on his or her account as needed during the month, for cash or to pay current bills. Whatever system you decide on, make the plan concrete and follow the agreed-upon procedure to avoid any misunderstanding.
- Finally, there is the very important monthly budget review. This review determines whether or not your program works. At this review, you and your partner check whether or not you are staying within budget limits. If not, decide what action to take to stop overspending— category by category. If you are underspending in some categories, you can adjust upward the budget limits in other account categories as good judgment advises.

A budget program as outlined here will provide reasonable assurance that you are spending your income wisely and in line with your preferences. Also, if you have planned well, you will know that allocations are being made regularly to your retirement and investment accounts to help ensure continued financial security.

Fourth Step: Saving and Investing

Let's move ahead to another important phase of financial planning: setting aside funds for savings and investments of some kind. The amount in your budget for this purpose may be small, but hopefully it will increase as you add a portion of your future cost-of-living and merit pay increases to the funds designated for savings.

Saving vs. Investing

What's the difference between saving and investing?

Saving means putting money away, typically for a short time horizon, for items such as a car, vacation or down payment on a house. Savings are usually put into safe places that allow you access to your money at any time. This often means there is low risk of losing the money, but the tradeoff is a low interest rate.

But how "safe" is a savings account if the interest it earns doesn't keep up with inflation? As an example, let's say you save a dollar. Today, that dollar can buy you a loaf of bread. But when you withdraw that dollar (plus the interest you earned) years later, and prices have gone up because of inflation, it might only be able to buy half a loaf. That is why many people put some of their money in savings but look to investing in an effort to earn more over longer periods of time.

Investing means putting some of your money away for the long term with the aim to make it grow by buying investment products that might increase in value, such as stocks or mutual funds. When investing, you have a greater chance of losing your money than when you save.

Many people just like you turn to the markets to help buy a home, send children to college or build a retirement nest egg. But unlike the banking world, where deposits are guaranteed by federal deposit insurance, the value of investments fluctuates with market conditions. No one can guarantee that you'll make money from your investments, and they may lose value. But you also have the opportunity to earn more money.

For most people, the only way to attain financial security is to save and invest over a long period of time. A key part of retirement planning is investing so that your money can grow. You just need to know a few basics, form a plan and be ready to stick to it.

Magic of Compounding

With compound interest, you earn interest on the money you save and on the interest that money earns. Over time, even a small amount saved can add up to big money.

Invest Each Month	Starting Age	Total Invested at Age 65	Total Value at Age 65
$200	35	$72,000	$166,452
$400	35	$144,000	$332,903
$200	45	$48,000	$82,206
$400	45	$96,000	$164,413
$200	55	$24,000	$31,056
$400	55	$48,000	$62,113

Figures are approximate based on annual return of investments of 5%. Factors to consider are taxes and inflation. Investments in a Roth IRA can be withdrawn tax-free.

You need to develop a plan for utilizing your savings effectively. Such a plan should provide for current day-to-day living expenses and emergency expenses, minimize credit card and loan debt, and make a start on setting aside money for major financial goals such as a home, vacation, special events, children, education and, ultimately, retirement.

Four Phases

This section covers the alternatives available for savings and investment purposes and how to structure a program. There are four phases in line with the way such a program is realistically developed:

- **First phase:** Setting aside an adequate checking and/or savings account and an emergency fund and getting basic insurance protection
- **Second phase:** Starting a savings program to meet your major financial goals

- **Third phase:** Expanding and increasing your investments
- **Fourth phase:** Using your retirement savings to fund your retirement years (decumulation).

Phase One: Adequate Funds and Protection

Everyone needs a bank account with an adequate balance to cover where your money goes each month for your monthly expenses. Your emergency fund, which ideally covers three to six months of income, should be in a separate account and used only for a financial emergency like sudden unemployment. These funds should be readily available. Still, even at this first phase, you want this fund to be earning something in the form of interest, likely an interest-earning savings account. Make sure that your local bank or credit union guarantees security of your emergency funds either by the Federal Deposit Insurance Corporation (FDIC) or the National

How Long Will Your Money Last?

This chart shows you how long your capital will last if you withdraw a fixed amount each year.

Percentage Withdrawn Yearly	Years Money Will Last if Invested at These Rates:					
	5%	6%	7%	8%	9%	10%
4%	*	*	*	*	*	*
8%	21	24	31	*	*	*
10%	15	16	18	21	27	*
12%	11	12	13	15	17	19
14%	10	10	11	12	12	14
16%	8	9	9	10	10	11
18%	7	7	8	8	9	9
20%	6	7	7	7	7	8

*This means your capital will last indefinitely at an annual interest rate that is the same as or equal to the amount you withdraw each year.

The goal is to have your money last as long as you do. Your budget should be able to respond to changes in investment performance, life expectancy and other factors.

Credit Union Administration (NCUA) and that your account totals less than the stipulated limit for liability.

Structuring Your Savings

The purpose of starting a savings and investment program is to provide financial security as the years go by—particularly in retirement. As we have emphasized, inflation makes this a particularly difficult goal to achieve.

Keep just enough in your checking to meet current monthly needs and the rest in savings or investment accounts that earn interest. Closely watch the balance between accounts to be sure you are earning interest on as much of your funds as possible.

Insurance Protection

If you're married or have a family, you must realize the need for life and disability insurance protection in the event that some unforeseen tragedy should befall you or your spouse. This need is greatest when you are younger since the insurance benefit must provide income for your family over many years. As you grow older, your policy may provide liquidity for your estate or pay your estate taxes.

Over the years, you should build assets that provide income protection. Set up your life insurance program early as part of your financial base. **(See "Life Insurance Options" on page 16.)**

With life insurance planning, the first thing to do is to consider what income the family would have, considering such factors as the earning ability of the surviving spouse, the current state of family finances, children's education, and the possibility and level of Social Security benefits. Set up your life insurance plan to come as close as possible to the monthly income needed for reasonably comfortable living.

You're twice as likely to be disabled for 90 days as to die before age 65. Yet fewer than half of all working adults have disability insurance.

How Much Money Do You Need to Save to Retire By Age 65?

According to researchers at the Stanford Center on Longevity, you need to put aside 10% to 17% of your income, even if you start saving as early as age 25. If you don't start saving until age 35 but still wish to retire at 65, then you need to contribute 15% to 20% of your income to your retirement accounts. If you have a pension, consider that a combined pension program and Social Security will generally replace about 60% of your preretirement income, so personal savings and still important.

- No matter your current age, you'll always be better off starting earlier than waiting until later.

- In your 40s and 50s, concentrate on financing retirement years. In your 40s, contribute enough to get your employer's maximum matching contribution. If you make Roth 401(k) or Roth IRA contributions now, that money may grow tax-free for ten to 20 years.

- In your 50s, you should have a good idea of what you're going to do in retirement and what adjustments you might have to make. Use a retirement calculator to see if your savings are on track. You can start making catch-up contributions to your retirement accounts at age 50.

- In your early 60s, you must begin thinking about when you will retire. How will you withdraw from your retirement funds to start paying yourself a retirement paycheck?

Life Insurance Options

Term life insurance provides the greatest dollar amount of death benefit for the least amount of money, and there is no risk of losing coverage during the policy term. The insurance coverage expires at the end of the policy term, commonly ten, 20 or 30 years.

You can buy a substantial amount of coverage for a relatively low price. However, the premiums for a specific amount of insurance become greater as you grow older. Term insurance does not build any cash value.

Permanent life insurance lasts as long as you pay your premiums. Premiums go toward both the death benefit and the cash value. The cash value is an investment-like feature. Be careful before purchasing. Investing in an insurance policy is expensive. Commissions, state taxes, required reserves, annual fees and early withdrawal penalties (if applicable) all reduce the investment. Understand the policy. Resist high-pressure sales pitches.

- **Whole life insurance** is the most common permanent option. Whole life provides a stipulated death benefit, level premiums and a cash value built at a fixed rate. You can borrow against this cash value and, if you eventually cancel the policy, cash it in, obtaining the savings that have built up. The drawback of this type of policy is the low interest rate on the cash value. On the plus side, there is a guaranteed minimum interest rate, so your cash value will grow similar to a savings account.

- **Universal life insurance** allows the policyholder to change the premium and death benefit amounts without getting a new policy. The cash value interest rate varies as market interest rates change. You can use the cash value to pay the premium. After 11 to 16 years, your policy could have sufficient cash value to pay the premium for the remainder of the policy.

- **Variable life insurance** combines the features of a whole life policy with those of a mutual fund. You can think of the cash value as invested in the stock market, making this option riskier than whole life insurance. The mutual fund-like feature means you can potentially get higher investment returns, but you can also lose money, depending on the market. There is a risk that your premium may be increased, and your death benefits may not be guaranteed.

A licensed life insurance representative or financial planner can help you figure out which option is best for you.

You and your spouse need enough coverage to maintain 60% to 70% of your current family income if either of you become disabled. Group disability coverage through your employer is cheapest. If that's not available, try to get a group rate through a group to which you belong.

The older you are when you apply for disability insurance, the higher the cost. You can lower costs by stretching the *elimination period*, which is the length of time you must wait before your benefits begin. A policy that starts payments on Day 90 of disability will cost 40% less than one that pays on Day 30.

For more information:
- **American Council of Life Insurers: Call (202) 624-2000, or go to www.acli.com.**
- **Insurance Information Institute: Call (212) 346-5500, or go to www.iii.org/insurance -basics/life-insurance.**

Phase Two: Major Financial Goals

Investors may have a wide range of goals they hope to achieve. What are the things you want to save and invest for? Some major goals include a home, car, wedding, vacation, education, retirement, future medical costs, and caring for parents and children. List your most important goals first. Decide how many years you have to meet each specific goal because when you save or invest, you'll need to find an option that fits your time frame. If you have a financial goal with a long time horizon, you may make more money by carefully investing in higher risk assets such as stocks than if you limit yourself to less risky assets. On the other hand, lower risk cash investments may be appropriate for short-term financial goals.

Building a Retirement Fund

Everyone should have some type of savings or investment program. It may involve only modest contributions but, if these contributions are consistently made into carefully selected, tax-efficient investments that provide decent returns and appreciation, it can help you to build funds for retirement.

When you talk about setting up a retirement fund, you discover that people fall into two categories:
- They work for a business or other type of organization.
- They are self-employed. **(See page 22.)**

Let's consider the investment approach appropriate to each of these groups.

Working for a Business

There are two approaches you can use to make your retirement fund tax-efficient:
- Participate in a company retirement program.
- Use an individual retirement account (IRA).

Your Employer's Plan

Employer retirement plans offer a lot of advantages to employees. Plans generally fall into two categories:
- *Defined benefit pension plan.* This type of plan promises you a specified monthly benefit at retirement. The employer shoulders the investment risks.
- *Defined contribution plan* such as a 401(k) or 403(b) plan. In these plans, you or your employer (or both) contribute to your individual account. The employee shoulders the investment risks, and the value of the account will fluctuate due to changes in the value of the investments. Upon retirement, you receive the balance in your account, which depends on contributions plus or minus investment gains or losses. **For more detail, go to www.ifebp.org /retirement101.**

Employer defined contribution plans are designed with a tax-efficient approach that is so important to decent growth in your investment savings. In some instances, your contributions to these plans are excluded from your earnings before income taxes are withheld. Usually, earnings on all types of contributions are sheltered from income taxes while they are held in the plan and until they are withdrawn.

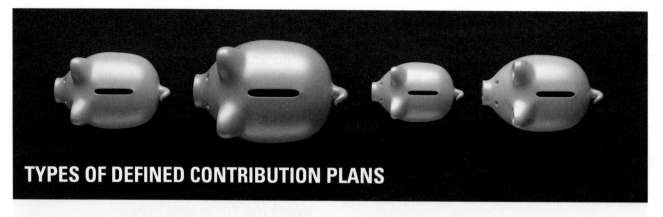

TYPES OF DEFINED CONTRIBUTION PLANS

401(k) plans give employees a choice of investment options, typically mutual funds. Employees who participate in a traditional 401(k) plan have a portion of their pretax salary invested directly in the option or options they choose. These contributions and any earnings from the 401(k) investments are not taxed until they are withdrawn.

Roth 401(k) plans are similar to a traditional plan, with one major exception. Contributions by employees are not tax-deferred but rather are made with after-tax dollars. Income earned on the account from interest, dividends or capital gains is tax-free.

Certain employers offer different tax-deferred retirement savings plans similar to 401(k) plans.

■ 403(b) plans are offered by employers such as public educational institutions (public schools, colleges and universities), certain nonprofits and religion-related organizations. Typically the plans offer two types of investment products: annuities and mutual funds.

■ 457(b) plans are offered by employers such as state and local government agencies and certain nonprofit organizations.

Profit-sharing plans allow employees to benefit from the money remaining after all costs of operating a business are paid. The employer contributions are discretionary; some years the employer contributes, some years the employer does not.

Money purchase plans require an employer contribution, usually a fixed percent of compensation per employee. Each employee has a separate account, and an employee's benefit is based on the amount of contributions to their account and the gains or losses associated with the account at the time of retirement.

For more information, go to www.investor .gov/introduction-investing/retirement-plans /employer-sponsored-plans.

Think of any employer match as free money. Employer matching means that your employer contributes a certain amount to your 401(k) account based on the amount you contribute. For example, for every dollar you contribute up to 6% of pay, your employer will contribute 50 cents. Just think:

A $200 monthly employee contribution to a 401(k) plan may qualify for a $100 matching contribution by the employer for a total of $300 monthly—$3,600 per year.

Those employer contributions will be yours once you're fully vested, which should be within six years of service at your company. Because of the advantages of your employer program, you should make every effort to participate by using the income set aside in your budget for retirement savings.

For many women, retirement is less financially secure than it is for men. On average, women live longer than men. Higher life expectancy means the average woman will have more retirement expenses than the average man. Despite this need for more retirement income, women tend to save less for retirement than men. Some reasons for this are, during their working years, women earn less on average and are more likely to leave the workforce or cut hours to care for children and parents. With lower career earnings, women receive less in Social Security benefits.

Surveys show the gender pay gap turns into a retirement savings gap for women. Women contribute less of their income to their 401(k) plan compared with men. According to a T. Rowe Price survey, Baby Boomer women have a median 401(k) savings balance of $59,000, less than half of the $138,000 median balance of Baby Boomer men. Millennial women have a median balance that is $30,000 less than that of Millennial men. **For more information, visit the National Resource Center on Women and Retirement Planning at www.wiserwomen.org /index.php?id=38.**

Individual Retirement Account (IRA)

If your employer does not have a retirement program, you will want to make an IRA your first choice for the investment of your retirement savings. Even if you do have a company program, you probably will want to contribute to an IRA to the extent possible if you have the funds to do so.

The two basic IRA types are traditional and Roth. Here are the main differences between them.

- Contributions to a traditional IRA are tax-deductible in the year they are made, and taxes are owed on distributions. Roth IRA contributions are not tax-deductible, but withdrawals are tax-free.
- The annual contribution limit is $6,000.
- For those age 50 and over, the maximum annual amount is $7,000. You must have earned income to cover your contribution.
- Beneficiaries may roll over retirement plan balances to their own retirement plan or traditional IRA.

- With a Roth IRA, contributions can be withdrawn without taxes or penalties after the account has been open for five years and after age 59½ or for death, disability, higher education or certain home purchases.
- With the traditional IRA, a tax-deferred plan, there is a 10% penalty for withdrawal prior to age 59½ except in the case of death, disability, higher education or certain home purchases.
- With a traditional IRA, you must start taking your required minimum distribution, determined by IRS, no later than April 1 of the year after you turn 70½. In a Roth IRA, you never have to withdraw your money. This can help in estate

FINDING LOST PENSIONS

Are you due a pension, but your old employer has gone out of business and you don't know where to go to collect your money? Help is available from the Pension Benefit Guaranty Corporation (PBGC) missing participant program: **www.pbgc.gov/search-unclaimed-pensions**

Search for your name (or the name of a beneficiary or relative who may be owed a benefit). If you find your name, you have two options. Complete the secure online form by clicking on the name of the missing participant. Be sure to include:

- Name
- Phone number
- Email address or mailing address.

You also can call 1-800-400-PBGC (7242) to speak to a member of the PBGC missing participant team or email missing@ pbgc.gov. For security purposes, if you send an email, do not include personal information such as your Social Security number, bank account numbers or address.

planning since a Roth IRA will allow you to leave tax-sheltered money to your heirs and avoid taking your required minimum distribution.

■ If you have a company 401(k) plan and you have stopped working for that company after you reach age 55, there will be no penalty for taking distributions from the plan. This does not apply to IRA accounts. To maintain this penalty-free distribution, the funds must not be rolled over into an IRA. Make sure you understand all the rules before starting

a distribution since it could result in costly mistakes. Also take into consideration how you will fund your many years in retirement.

■ Anyone can convert a traditional IRA to a Roth IRA. When you convert from an IRA to a Roth IRA, you owe ordinary income tax on the converted amount. You should have enough money to pay the tax with other funds. If you pay with the funds in the IRA, it would be considered a premature distribution subject to a 10% penalty.

Feature Comparisons of Retirement Accounts

Feature	Roth 401(k)	Roth IRA	Traditional 401(k)
Contributions	Roth employee elective contributions are made with *after-tax dollars.*	Roth IRA contributions are made with *after-tax dollars.*	Traditional, pretax employee elective contributions are made with *pretax dollars.*
Income Limits	No income limitation to participate	Married phaseout starts at $196,000; ineligible at $206,000. Single phaseout starts at $124,000; ineligible at $139,000 (modified AGI).	No income limitation to participate
Maximum Elective Contributions	Combined* employee elective contributions limited to $19,500 ($26,000 for employees age 50 or over)	Contribution limited to $6,000 ($7,000 for employees age 50 or over)	Same combined* limit as Roth 401(k) account
Taxation Withdrawals	Withdrawals of contributions and earnings are not taxed provided they are a qualified distribution—The account is held for at least five years and made because of disability, death or the attainment of age 59½.	Same as Roth 401(k) account; there can be a qualified distribution for a first-time home purchase.	Withdrawals of contributions and earnings are subject to federal and most state income taxes.
Required Distributions	Distributions must begin no later than age 70½ unless still working and not a 50% owner.	No requirement to start taking distributions while owner is alive	Same as Roth 401(k) account

This limitation is by individual rather than by plan. Although it is permissible to split the annual employee elective contribution between designated Roth contributions and traditional pretax contributions, the combination cannot exceed the deferral limit.

Source: Internal Revenue Service.

Third Phase: Expanding Investments

The purpose of this phase of your investment planning is to increase your savings to the point that they will provide for any additional needs and preferences: advanced education for the children, a better home, the possibility of travel now and in retirement, etc.

Ideally, your personal situation at this point is that your income from work has increased and/or you have multiple incomes in your household.

For retirement and whatever types of investments you decide to use, you will want to emphasize certain approaches with your contributions.

- Make your yearly investment as large as possible, considering the money you have available.
- Make your contribution procedure as painless as possible by setting it up as an automatic payroll deduction or as an automatic payment from your bank account.

Consistent contributions are an important factor in building substantial investments over the years. This approach has the added advantage of letting you *dollar average* your stock or fund purchases, a process that tends to hold down the average cost of shares, which continually fluctuate in price.

You continue to live on your budget (somewhat modified, of course) so that funds are not being wasted. Now, you should look beyond the basic start you have made in your employer retirement plan or IRA to a more extensive form of investment.

SIMPLE SAVINGS TIPS

- Take advantage of any employer retirement programs. Contribute at least enough to get your employer's full match. Money in these accounts is there for retirement. Resist any urge to withdraw it for a purpose other than retirement.

- Have a separate savings account. Automatically deposit part of your paycheck here.

- Do not spend your next raise.

- If you get a tax refund or bonus, save it.

- Pay off your mortgage sooner by making extra payments on the principal.

- Pay off credit cards, highest interest rate first, to save the money you now spend on interest charges.

- Ask to have all dividends from mutual funds or stocks automatically reinvested.

- Contribute to an IRA.

- Save early. Thanks to compounding, $1,000 saved this year will have far greater value when you retire than the same $1,000 put away ten or 20 years from now.

- Trim your spending.

Sound Investment Principles

Before discussing investments further, it's important to understand and consider some key concepts and terms.

- **Time horizon:** This means the length of time you expect to keep your money invested. For a short-term investment goal (five years or less), you don't want to choose risky investments, because when it's time to sell, you may have to take a loss. With a longer time horizon, you may feel more comfortable taking on riskier investments that are able to ride out difficult markets and appreciate over a long period of time.

- **Economic conditions:** The longer investment horizon you have, the less attention you need to pay to the economy. People who stay invested with consistent contributions are better able to weather economic downturns. Do not attempt to time the market.

- **Asset allocation:** Asset allocation involves dividing your investments among different assets, such as stocks, bonds and cash. The allocation that works best for you changes at different times in your life, depending on how long you have to invest and your ability to tolerate risk.
- **Risk tolerance:** When it comes to investing, risk and reward go hand in hand. The phrase "no pain, no gain" comes close to summing up the relationship between risk and reward. All investments involve some degree of risk. If you plan to buy securities—such as stocks, bonds and mutual funds—it's important that you understand that you could lose some or all of the money you invest. An aggressive investor, or one with a high risk tolerance, is willing to risk losing money to get potentially better results. A conservative investor, or one with a low risk tolerance, favors investments that maintain his or her original investment.
- **Diversified investments:** Experts agree on one thing: The best way to cut your investment risk is to diversify. Diversification can be neatly summed up as, "Don't put all your eggs in one basket." The idea is that if one investment loses money, the other investments will make up for those losses. Diversification can't guarantee that your investments won't suffer if the market drops. But it can improve the chances that you won't lose money or that, if you do, it won't be as much as if you weren't diversified.
- **Quality investments:** Carefully select the funds and sources in which you plan to invest. Comparison shop, and explore alternatives. Be particularly careful of fees, loads and commissions.
- **Minimum administrative costs:** Look for no-load, minimum-cost investments, and avoid turning over your investments more often than necessary.

In applying these investment principles, there generally are two different approaches to take.
- Use a financial planner.
- Do it yourself.

IF YOU ARE SELF-EMPLOYED

Those who are self-employed have many of the same options to save for retirement on a tax-advantaged basis as employees participating in company plans. Your options include:

- Simplified employee pension (SEP)
- 401(k) plan
- Savings Incentive Match Plan for Employees (SIMPLE).

For more information, go to www.irs.gov /retirement-plans/retirement-plans-for-self -employed-people.

Using a Financial Planner

There are two types of financial planners: those who are affiliated with investment products and paid commissions and those who are *fee-only*, which means they do not accept fees based on selling investment products.

Although financial planners can help you make investment decisions, hiring a planner presumes you have discretionary income to invest. Experts say most investments should not be made until you have financed very basic living items, such as housing, insurance and an emergency fund. If you find you cannot meet these (and other) necessary financial requirements, you may decide you need help not in investment planning but in basic money management.

Whether or not you use the services of a financial planner, you must organize by preparing your own net worth and cash flow worksheets. Be informed on financial matters. Your local educational institutions may offer classes.

A financial planner should help not only with your investments, including creating a retirement strategy, but also with your insurance and estate planning.

Be careful when choosing a financial planner. Be cautious about free retirement planning seminars because the presenters may make misleading claims about the investment products they are affiliated with. Contact your state securities department to verify that an advisor is registered. Confirm the advisor does not have any complaints by using www.brokercheck.finra.org.

Interview three or four advisors to find out if they are a good match for you. Before choosing a financial planner, ask questions.

- What are your qualifications?
- What can you sell me?
- May I talk with other clients like me?
- How do you get paid? By commission? By the amount of assets you manage? By another method?
- Do I have any choice on how to pay you? Should I pay you by the transaction or pay a flat fee regardless of how many transactions I have?

If you need a financial planner, get recommendations from other financial professionals, such as an insurance agent or lawyer, and ask your friends and colleagues. Or you can find one through industry associations.

The Financial Planning Association offers fee-only planners who have at least two years of experience and at least one professional designation. Call (800) 322-4237, or visit www .plannersearch.org.

The National Association of Personal Financial Advisors has a directory of fee-only advisors. Call (847) 483-5400, or visit www .napfa.org.

Find a CFP Certified Financial Planner™ at www.letsmakeaplan.org.

The Do-It-Yourself (DIY) Approach

Some people like personal control of their investments and choose to build their own portfolio of assets. This takes dedication and thorough research. If you have an employer retirement plan like a 401(k), even if you don't

like the limited investment choices, contribute enough to get the maximum matching contribution. Once you're contributing enough to earn that match, you can consider investing through other accounts. Here are the basic types of accounts for DIY investing.

- *Brokerage accounts* are taxable accounts you open with a brokerage company to buy investments. You transfer money to the account and make your investment choices. Brokerage accounts offer you access to the full range of investment products, including more complicated options. There are many online brokerage companies.
- *Fund family accounts* are an option for investors who choose to build portfolios of open-end mutual funds transacted directly with the fund company.
- *Robo-advisors* offer investors a passive option to automate portfolios that are built on modern portfolio theory. Robo-advisors typically have a low fee compared with human advisors.
- *Self-directed individual retirement accounts* are available through specialized companies. They have the same tax advantages, restrictions and contribution limits as traditional IRAs.

RISK TOLERANCE QUESTIONNAIRES

Your employer plan servicer may offer a free questionnaire to help you assess your risk tolerance. If not, many investment websites offer free questionnaires. Some of the websites will even estimate asset allocations based on responses to the questionnaires. While the suggested asset allocations may be a useful starting point, keep in mind that the results may be biased toward financial products or services sold by companies or individuals sponsoring the websites.

LEARN ABOUT INVESTMENT OPTIONS

The U.S. **Securities and Exchange Commission (SEC)** enforces the laws on how investments are offered and sold to you. A security is any proof of ownership or debt that has been assigned a value and may be sold. SEC website www.investor.gov provides unbiased information to help you evaluate your choices.

Be careful. Keep your financial goals in mind. Do not attempt to time the market. DIY investors may make emotional decisions instead of logical ones. It's human nature. Most investors buy and sell at the wrong times. Dalbar, an independent research firm that has studied mutual fund investor behavior, found that the average mutual fund investor has underperformed the stock market, while investors in bond mutual funds haven't kept up with inflation. Why? For investments with long time horizons, emotions make it difficult to follow the rules of buy low, sell high; stay invested in diversified low-cost index funds. Dalbar found that variable annuity investors outperformed mutual fund investors, likely because the variable annuity surrender charges were a motivation to be disciplined despite emotions and to leave the money invested for a long period even during market downturns.

Learn About Investment Options

Stocks, bonds, mutual funds and exchange-traded funds (ETFs) are the most common asset categories. These are among the asset categories you would likely choose from when investing in a retirement savings program or a college savings plan. Do not invest in something you do not understand.

Here's a list of the main categories of investments on a continuum from low risk to higher risk.

- **Certificates of deposit (CDs):** A certificate of deposit (CD) is a savings account that holds a fixed amount of money for a fixed period of time—such as six months, one year or five years—and, in exchange, the issuing bank pays interest. When you cash in your CD, you receive the money you originally invested plus any interest. CDs have a long-standing reputation as low-risk investments. CDs offer higher interest rates than regular savings accounts and can be easily converted to cash. A CD bought through a federally insured bank is insured up to $250,000. Brokered CDs from brokerage firms are very different. Some have variable interest rates. Some take decades to mature. Some give the brokerage firm the right to terminate the CD but do not give that right to the investor. If the investor needs money before the CD matures, the only option is to sell the CD back to the broker, often at a significant loss.
- **Bonds:** This is a certificate of debt similar to an IOU issued by a company, government or municipality. Borrowers issue bonds to raise money from investors willing to lend them money for a certain amount of time. When you buy a bond, you are lending to the issuer. In return, the issuer promises to pay you a specified interest rate during the life of the bond and to repay the principal when it matures or comes due after a set period of time. Overall, bonds are considered relatively low-risk investments.
- **Mutual funds:** A mutual fund is a company that brings together money from many people and invests it in stocks, bonds or other assets. There are many kinds of mutual funds. For example, bond funds invest primarily in bonds, while stock funds invest primarily in stocks.
- **Balanced funds:** These funds invest in stocks and bonds and sometimes money market funds in an attempt to reduce risk but still provide capital appreciation and income. Balanced funds are designed to reduce risk by diversifying among investment categories, but they still

share the same risks that are associated with the underlying types of instruments.

- **Money market funds:** Money market funds invest in highly liquid, low-risk securities such as government bonds, CDs and *commercial paper* (short-term unsecured promissory notes issued by companies).

- **ETFs:** Like mutual funds, ETFs offer investors a way to pool their money in a fund that makes investments in stocks, bonds or other assets and, in return, to receive an interest in that investment pool. Unlike mutual funds, however, ETF shares are traded on a national stock exchange, with price changes throughout the day as the ETF is bought and sold. Initially, ETFs were all designed to track the performance of specific U.S. equity indexes; most ETFs trading in the marketplace are index-based ETFs. Newer ETFs, however, also seek to track indexes of fixed-income instruments and foreign securities. In addition, newer ETFs include ETFs that are actively managed—that is, they do not merely seek to passively track an index; instead, they seek to achieve a specified investment objective using an active investment strategy.

- **Index funds:** Index funds are types of mutual funds or exchange-traded funds that seek to track the returns of a market index. A *market index* measures the performance of a basket of securities (like stocks or bonds). The Standard and Poor's (S&P) 500 Index and the Russell 2000 Index are examples of market indexes. Because index funds generally use a *passive investing strategy,* which means they aim to maximize returns over the long run by not buying and selling securities very often, they may be able to save costs. Since the overall trend of stock market prices over the long run has been up, this characteristic should be advantageous in the long run.

- **Target-date funds:** Sometimes referred to as lifecycle funds, target-date funds, which are often mutual funds, hold a mix of stocks, bonds and other investments. Over time, the mix gradually shifts according to the fund's investment strategy. Target-date funds are designed to be long-term investments for individuals with particular retirement dates in mind. The name of the fund often refers to its target date. For example, you might see funds with names like "Portfolio 2030," "Retirement Fund 2030" or "Target 2030" that are designed for individuals who intend to retire in or near the year 2030. Most target-date funds are designed so that the fund's mix of investments will automatically change in a way that is

WHAT'S THE DIFFERENCE BETWEEN ACTIVE AND PASSIVE INVESTING?

An active investment strategy relies on the skill of an investment manager who aims to outperform an investment benchmark or index. An actively managed fund has the potential to outperform the market, but its performance is dependent on the skill of the manager. Also, actively managed funds historically have had higher management fees, which can significantly lower investment returns.

Passive investing is an investment strategy that is designed to achieve approximately the same return as a particular market index, before fees. Index funds are an example of passively managed mutual funds. Most ETFs are also passively managed. Passive investing typically comes with lower management fees.

intended to become more conservative as you approach the target date. Typically, the funds shift over time from a mix with a lot of stock investments in the beginning to a mix weighted more toward bonds. Target-date funds are often available through 401(k) plans. Some 401(k) plans use these funds as the default investment for plan participants who have not selected their investments under the plan.

- **Stocks:** Stocks are a type of security that gives stockholders a share of ownership in a company. Stocks also are called equities. Investors buy stocks for various reasons. Here are some of them:
  - Capital appreciation, which occurs when a stock rises in price
  - Dividend payments, which come when the company distributes some of its earnings to stockholders
  - Ability to vote shares and influence the company.

Stocks offer investors the greatest potential for growth (capital appreciation) over the long haul. Investors willing to stick with stocks over long periods of time, say 15 years, generally have been rewarded with strong, positive returns. But stock prices move down as well as up. There's no guarantee that the company whose stock you hold will grow and do well, so you can lose money you invest in stocks. **For more information, go to: www.investor.gov/introduction-investing.**

Annuities

An *annuity* is a contract between you and an insurance company that requires the insurer to make payments to you, either immediately or in the future. You buy an annuity by making either a single payment or a series of payments. Similarly, your payout may come either as one lump-sum payment or as a series of payments over time.

There are three basic types of annuities:

- **Fixed annuity:** The insurance company promises you a minimum rate of interest and a fixed amount of periodic payments.

- **Variable annuity:** The insurance company allows you to direct your annuity payments to different investment options, usually mutual funds. Your payout will vary depending on how much you put in, the rate of return on your investments, and expenses. The SEC regulates variable annuities. **For more information, go to www.sec.gov/investor/pubs/sec-guide-to -variable-annuities.pdf.**

- **Indexed annuity:** This annuity combines features of securities and insurance products. The insurance company credits you with a return that is based on a stock market index.

Fourth Phase: Decumulation

You've accumulated retirement savings for some or all of your working life. *Decumulation* is using the money in your retirement savings account to live off of in retirement. If you have a defined benefit plan, you'll often have a choice among three distribution options: a payment schedule that lasts the lifetime of the employee, a payment schedule that lasts the lifetimes of both the employee and a spouse, or a lump-sum distribution.

Lump-Sum Distributions

If you have participated in a 401(k) or any other qualified retirement plan for three years, you may have the option of receiving a lump-sum distribution upon leaving employment for a job change or retirement. If your account has a balance of $1,000 to $5,000, your employer will deposit this directly into an IRA unless otherwise directed.

Choosing the lump sum isn't the best decision for most people. Before taking the lump sum in cash, you should consider your life expectancy and the potential needs of your surviving spouse. A lump-sum distribution is usually the entire balance in your retirement savings plan. Since this could be a large sum, you should consult a tax advisor to help you decide among the available options.

Basically, you can take the distribution as ordinary income and pay taxes on it the year it is received (no tax is due on your after-tax contributions), or you can defer taxation by rolling over all or part of the money into an individual retirement account (IRA). Other alternatives for your distribution include keeping it invested in stock, buying an individual retirement annuity or leaving it in your employer's plan.

In determining the best course of action, consider the amount of the distribution, how soon you need the money, other resources available to you, your age, your health, your family and your anticipated investment returns. Research your options, and be careful.

Option 1: Take Cash

You have the option to take the entire lump sum in cash. This is not the best option for most people. Taxes must be paid on the amount received (excluding any after-tax contributions). If you are under age 59½, you may incur a 10% penalty for early withdrawal.

Employers must withhold 20% from eligible rollover distributions for federal income taxes unless the money is directly rolled over to an IRA or another qualified retirement plan.

You may be able to minimize your tax bite, but it becomes complicated. Consult with a tax accountant before you take the money.

Option 2: Roll It Into an IRA

You can defer paying income taxes on all or part of a lump-sum distribution by reinvesting the money in an IRA through a direct or indirect rollover. (After-tax contributions made after 2001 can be transferred.)

In order to avoid having 20% of your distribution withheld, you should request a direct rollover to an IRA (trust to trust). With this approach, you instruct your employer to directly roll your distribution into an IRA rather than

INVESTMENT FEES

As with anything you buy, there are fees and costs associated with investment products and services. These fees may seem small, but over time they can have a major impact on your investment portfolio. Understanding the fees you pay is important to investing wisely.

- What are the total fees to purchase, maintain and sell this investment?

- Are there ways that I can reduce or avoid some of the fees I'll pay, such as by purchasing the investment directly?

- How much does this investment have to increase in value before I break even?

- What are the ongoing fees to maintain my account?

- For mutual funds: How much will the fund charge me when I buy and/or sell shares?

Fees reduce the value of your investment return. If the holdings of two funds have identical performance, the fund with the lower fees generally will generate higher returns for you. Even small differences in fees can translate into large differences in returns over time. For example, if you invested $10,000 in a fund that produced a 5% annual return before expenses and had annual operating expenses of 1.5%, then after 20 years you would have roughly $19,612. But if the fund had expenses of only 0.5%, then you would end up with $24,002—a 23% difference.

Use a mutual fund cost calculator to see how the costs of different mutual funds add up over time and eat into your returns. Visit FINRA Fund Analyzer at https://tools.finra.org/fund_analyzer.

Saving for Education

If you have children or grandchildren you hope will pursue education beyond high school, planning for college is important, especially since college tuitions are rising. When deciding the best way to save for college, remember that there are grants and loans available for college but not for your retirement plan. One option is to save in a savings account. When the time comes and you have the means, you can help pay for college; otherwise, you have this savings as a safety net for retirement or emergencies.

If tax savings are important to you, there are some tax benefits for college savings. The Federal Student Aid office of the Department of Education offers an overview at www.studentaid.ed.gov/sa/types/tax-benefits.

- **Section 529 College Savings Plans**
  529 plans are established by a state or school so that you can either prepay or save up to pay education-related expenses with tax-free withdrawals. For more information, go to www.collegesavings.org.

- **Coverdell Education Savings Account**
  Allows up to $2,000 a year to be put aside for a student's education expenses (elementary, secondary or college). For more information, go to www.savingforcollege.com/intro_to_esas.

- **Roth IRA**
  A Roth IRA is intended to be a retirement account but can be used for education. Your contributions can be withdrawn tax-free and without penalty at any time for any reason. Earnings in the account are different: Earnings that you use for college tuition will be taxed as income. Once you turn 59½, you can withdraw the earnings tax-free.

pay the money to you. Make sure it is payable to the custodian of your new IRA. Otherwise, the distribution will be subject to the 20% withholding and maybe penalties.

If the distribution is paid to you, you can still do an indirect rollover, but you must reinvest the money in an IRA within 60 days. However, even if you roll over the total amount received, you will pay income taxes, as well as a possible 10% penalty if you're under age 59½, on the 20% of the distribution withheld by your employer. To avoid

this, you must roll over the 20% from your own pocket.

With this option, you must begin to take your required minimum distribution, determined by the IRS, at age 70½.

Option 3: Keep the Stock

If your retirement plan consists mostly of highly appreciated stock, it might be a good idea to keep the company stock. Talk to a trusted financial advisor. Keep in mind that the principle underlying good retirement planning is diversification. Do not put all your eggs in one basket. Although you can get favorable tax treatment by keeping company stock, it must not be the overriding consideration.

You will owe taxes, but only on the value of the shares at the time you purchased them or when the company added them to your account. You can continue to defer taxes on all the share-price gains from the initial date of purchase until you sell the stock. You will pay annual income taxes on any dividends.

In doing this, you convert what might have been ordinary income into long-term capital gain. Your heirs may fare better with this option since they will owe taxes only on the share-price gain of the stock prior to taking the shares out of the plan.

To find out how much you might save in taxes, ask your employee benefits department to provide you with the net unrealized appreciation (NUA) on those shares before you make any withdrawals.

Option 4: Take a Lifetime Annuity

Many plans offer annuity distributions. Should you desire an annuity, it's probably a better value to obtain one through your employer's plan.

People typically buy annuities to help manage their income in retirement. Annuities provide three things:

- Periodic payments for a specific amount of time. This may be for the rest of your life or the life of your spouse or another person.
- Death benefits. If you die before you start receiving payments, the person you name as your beneficiary receives a specific payment.

- Tax-deferred growth. You pay no taxes on the income and investment gains from your annuity until you withdraw the money.

Annuities are complicated and are only suitable for long-term financial goals. Be careful.

There are sales commissions, fees and charges that affect your return. Most annuities have severance charges if you withdraw within a certain period, usually up to seven years. Also, under most circumstances, there will be a 10% penalty on the interest you have earned for a withdrawal that occurs before age 59½. Learn all you can about annuities before purchasing.

Option 5: Employer Plan

You may choose to leave the lump sum in your employer's plan. Check with your employee benefits department. If they allow former participants to keep their accounts, the likely result is lower costs to you and, thus, higher returns. Remember, if you roll over your lump sum, you become an individual investor and may encounter charges such as fees and commissions— two things normally not present in the employer's plan. Be careful about diversification. Be aware that investments may be moved without your permission.

Option 6: New Employment

If you switch employment from a nonprofit or government job to the private sector or vice versa, the 2001 Tax Act allows you to roll your tax-deferred retirement savings vehicles, including 403(b) plans, some 457 plans and traditional IRAs, to your new employer's retirement plan.

Checklist for
Financial Preparation

When you are planning for future finances, here are some questions to ask yourself.

Have you . . .
Yes No

○ ○ Put all your vital financial records in one place, told someone else where they are and made copies of them?

○ ○ Reviewed your expenses and savings at least once a year?

○ ○ Paid down your high-interest debt and paid off your mortgage and car payments?

○ ○ Created an adequate savings fund whose purpose is to provide money for day-to-day living and manage debt?

○ ○ Created an adequate emergency fund with three to six months of income?

○ ○ Obtained life and disability insurance plans that provide adequate protection at a competitive cost—particularly during early family years?

○ ○ Identified your financial goals?

○ ○ Created a savings and investment plan based on your goals?

○ ○ Created your investment plan with an understanding of your time horizon and risk tolerance?

○ ○ Used employer retirement plans, such as 401(k)s, and maxed out any employer match?

○ ○ Made consistent contributions to a savings and investment program to build up to significant levels over the years?

○ ○ Researched all investments thoroughly and maintained a diversified portfolio?

○ ○ Figured your retirement expenses, keeping inflation in mind, identified financial assets and projected their growth before retirement?

○ ○ Talked over retirement finances with your spouse or, if you are single, with someone close to you?

If you checked any item "No," you know where you need to do some work.

Quick Financial Overview

The first step in financial planning is to figure out where you stand today. Take a few moments to fill out this worksheet. Don't spend a lot of time digging through records or being exact. Just make your best estimate for each category. You will want to do a more careful analysis later (see the worksheets on pages 32-34). You may be surprised at your financial status. This will give you a basis for your financial and retirement planning.

Monthly Income

Monthly wages/salary $ _____

Dividends/interest $ _____

Other $ _____

TOTAL MONTHLY INCOME $ _____

Monthly Expenses

Mortgage/rent $ _____

Transportation $ _____

Food $ _____

Education $ _____

Child care $ _____

Entertainment/recreation $ _____

Loans (car/credit card, etc.) $ _____

Utilities (gas, phone, electricity, water, etc.) $ _____

Miscellaneous (clothes, insurance, medical, etc.) $ _____

TOTAL MONTHLY EXPENSES $ _____

Monthly Income $ _____

– (minus) Monthly Expenses $ _____

+ (plus) Savings and Investments $ _____

= (equals) TOTAL DISCRETIONARY CASH $ _____

Retirement Expense Worksheet

Step 1: Using this worksheet, record everything you spend for one month. If you have some expenses that don't fit any category, include them at the bottom.

Step 2: To determine your yearly expenses, multiply your monthly expenses by 12.

Step 3: To determine your projected yearly retirement expenses, multiply your yearly expenses by 0.90. The result is an approximation of how much you'll need per year during retirement, not factoring in inflation.

Housing
(rent or mortgage, property/real estate taxes, household maintenance) $ _____

Essentials
(food, clothing, medical and dental bills) $ _____

Taxes
(income, property, Social Security) $ _____

Utilities
(gas, electric, telephone) $ _____

Transportation
(car loans, gas, car maintenance, plane, train, bus and taxi fares) $ _____

Leisure
(vacation home mortgage, entertainment, travel, club dues) $ _____

Loan and installment payments
(bank, auto, home equity loans, credit card debt) $ _____

Insurance
(health, auto, homeowner, life, long-term care) $ _____

Gifts, charitable contributions $ _____

TOTAL MONTHLY EXPENSES $ _____

(multiply by 12)   × 12

= TOTAL YEARLY EXPENSES $ _____

(multiply by 0.90)   × 0.90

= TOTAL YEARLY RETIREMENT EXPENSES $ _____

Cash Flow Worksheet

Date:_____

	Last Year	In Retirement
INCOME		
Wages or salary	$ _____	$ _____
Additional household wages or salary	$ _____	$ _____
Dividends and interest	$ _____	$ _____
Child support/alimony	$ _____	$ _____
Annuities, pensions, Social Security	$ _____	$ _____
Rents, royalties, fees	$ _____	$ _____
Other _____	$ _____	$ _____
TOTAL INCOME	$ _____	$ _____
TAXES		
Income taxes	$ _____	$ _____
Social Security/Medicare taxes	$ _____	$ _____
Property taxes	$ _____	$ _____
Other _____	$ _____	$ _____
TOTAL TAXES	$ _____	$ _____
LIVING EXPENSES		
Rent or mortgage payments	$ _____	$ _____
Food	$ _____	$ _____
Clothing	$ _____	$ _____
Utilities	$ _____	$ _____
Meals out	$ _____	$ _____
Furniture and other durable goods	$ _____	$ _____
Recreation, entertainment, vacations	$ _____	$ _____
Gasoline	$ _____	$ _____
Car payments	$ _____	$ _____
Financial and legal services	$ _____	$ _____
Doctor, drugs, medical expenses	$ _____	$ _____
Interest	$ _____	$ _____
Household maintenance	$ _____	$ _____
Car repairs	$ _____	$ _____
Tuition/day care	$ _____	$ _____
Health care, life and disability insurance premiums	$ _____	$ _____
Grooming (i.e., laundry, cleaning)	$ _____	$ _____
Medications	$ _____	$ _____
Auto insurance premiums	$ _____	$ _____
Health insurance premiums	$ _____	$ _____
Other (i.e., gifts)	$ _____	$ _____
TOTAL ANNUAL LIVING EXPENSES	$ _____	$ _____
FUNDS AVAILABLE FOR SAVINGS AND INVESTMENTS (total income minus taxes and living expenses)	$ _____	$ _____

Net Worth Worksheet

Date:_____

Property Assets *

Residence $_____

Vacation home $_____

Furnishings $_____

Jewelry/art $_____

Automobiles $_____

Other $_____

Equity Assets *

Real estate $_____

Stocks $_____

Mutual funds $_____

Variable annuity $_____

Business equity $_____

Other $_____

Cash Reserve Assets *

Checking account $_____

Savings account $_____

Credit union $_____

CDs $_____

Other $_____

Fixed Assets *

Government bonds $_____

Municipal bonds $_____

Corporate bonds $_____

Fixed annuities $_____

Other $_____

TOTAL ASSETS $_____

Liabilities **

Home mortgage $_____

Other mortgage $_____

Bank loans $_____

Auto loans $_____

Personal loans $_____

Credit card debt $_____

Other $_____

TOTAL LIABILITIES $_____

TOTAL ASSETS $_____

– (minus) TOTAL LIABILITIES $_____

= (equals) YOUR NET WORTH *** $_____

This is your personal financial overview. You may be surprised at your net worth, especially if your home has appreciated significantly in value or if you have significant loans or credit card debt. Your cash flow and your net worth will provide the starting point for your financial future. By managing your cash flow, you can build your net worth and turn your dreams into realities.

· ·

*For calculation of your assets, use current value, not the original purchase price.

**Amounts due (not monthly installments but total balances) in accounts with credit card companies, department stores and other retailers and to anyone else to whom you owe money. This is an important total to know and to review periodically; many who run into credit problems do so because they have lost track of how much they owe overall— It's too easy to charge.

***To compute your net worth, total your liabilities and deduct this amount from your total assets (if the amount is larger, you're facing trouble). The result is your net worth. After you've done this one, subsequent surveys will be easier; you will have basic figures that will only need reviewing and adjusting. A 20% increase in net worth annually is considered ideal—but don't really expect such a gain until later years.

Social Security

"Aging is not lost youth but a new stage of opportunity and strength."

—Betty Friedan

One Part of Retirement Planning

Social Security is an important financial component of retirement planning for most people. Some 64 million benefit payments go out each month. Social Security is essentially a family program that offers these major benefits:

- Retirement benefits
- Survivor benefits
- Disability benefits
- Medicare benefits.

Benefits can also be paid to dependents of retired, disabled or deceased workers (refer to the dependent benefits chart on page 41). Each of the major benefits will be discussed in more detail later. Social Security acts as a kind of insurance at important junctures in your family's life: retirement, disability and death.

How You Qualify

For any benefits to be paid, the worker must have worked long enough and sometimes recently enough to qualify (also known as being fully insured). Work in jobs covered by Social Security earns quarters of coverage (or credits). Four credits

can be earned in a calendar year. Before 1978, a worker had to actually earn $50 or more during a calendar quarter to earn a credit. Beginning in 1978, yearly credits are determined by the amount of your earnings. These increments increase every year. In 2020, one credit is earned for each $1,341; therefore, $5,640 will earn the four-credit maximum for the calendar year.

Not all employees work in jobs covered by Social Security. For example, most federal employees hired before 1984 and employees of some state and local governments that chose not to participate in Social Security are in noncovered work.

The number of credits needed depends on the type of benefit involved. As a rule of thumb, one credit is needed for each year after age 21 up to the year of age 62, death or disability. It does not matter when the credits are earned.

Some people think that their Social Security benefits will be based on the number of credits they have. This is not true. The dollar amount of any benefits paid has nothing to do with the number of credits you have. You either qualify or do not qualify for benefits based on credits. The calculation of the benefit amount uses your lifetime earnings.

Is Your Record Accurate?

The Social Security Administration has been keeping records of your earnings throughout your working life. Are those records accurate and up to date? Imagine filing for your benefits and finding them shortchanged or delayed because of errors made years ago.

Check your records: Each year, check your W-2 (Wage and Tax Statement) to make sure your employer has your name and Social Security number correct. **To get your benefit estimate, go to www.ssa.gov/benefits/retirement/estimator.html, call (800) 772-1213 or set up your free, personal account at www.ssa.gov/myaccount.** Social Security mails annual benefit statements to workers age 60 and over who aren't receiving Social Security benefits and haven't set up an account. At least every three years, request a statement of your earnings from Social Security. Review your statement carefully, and report any errors immediately to the Social Security Administration. Save any electronic communications. If you communicate to someone in person or over the phone, note the date, time and name of the person you spoke with in your own records.

Check for overpayments: You may also find that an employer did not stop collecting Social Security taxes after reaching the maximum taxable amount in a given year or that you worked for more than one employer in a year and your total wages exceeded the maximum. You can receive a refund or a credit against your federal income tax. Request it on your income tax return.

Age to Receive Full Retirement Benefits*

Year of Birth	Full Retirement Age (FRA)*
1941	65 and 8 months
1942	65 and 10 months
1943-54	66
1955	66 and 2 months
1956	66 and 4 months
1957	66 and 6 months
1958	66 and 8 months
1959	66 and 10 months
1960 and later	67

This chart does not apply to survivor benefits.

*If you take monthly benefits before FRA, your benefits are reduced. Medicare is still available at age 65, regardless of FRA.

Retirement Benefits

When to start receiving Social Security retirement benefits is a personal choice. Base your decision on your circumstances. Factors to consider include your current cash needs, your current health, family longevity, future expenses, future health care needs, whether you plan to work in retirement and how much you've saved in your retirement fund.

Very few people find their Social Security checks sufficient to cover their expenses. The program is designed to replace 40% or less of preretirement wages for most retirees, and that's not enough for a comfortable life in retirement. **(See the chart on page 38 for estimates of Social Security wage replacement.)** Most experts suggest a comfortable replacement would total around 80% to 100% or more of your preretirement wages. The chart shows that Social Security is a small portion of the total retirement income you will need.

Find out what you can expect from Social Security and how it will fit into your retirement plans. Your Social Security retirement benefits will be based on your lifetime earnings—specifically, your 35 highest paid years of earnings are averaged together to determine a benefit amount, called the *primary insurance amount* (PIA).

For an explanation of how retirement benefits are figured, ask Social Security for the fact sheet Your Retirement Benefit: How It's Figured, or visit www.ssa.gov/pubs/EN-05-10070.pdf.

The calculations to figure Social Security retirement benefits are gender-neutral. Women and men who have identical work records and earn identical amounts would receive an identical benefit from Social Security. In reality, women often receive smaller benefit amounts than men for a few reasons. First, because of the gender pay gap, women's earnings are often lower than men's. Second, men are more likely to have a steady work history because women are more likely to interrupt careers for caregiving. A year without working for pay is counted as $0, which brings down the average lifetime earnings, thereby bringing down the benefits.

For more information, go to:
- **www.ssa.gov/people/women**
- **What Every Woman Should Know: www.ssa .gov/pubs/EN-05-10127.pdf.**

As a quick check on the funds you can look forward to receiving at FRA, consider what percentage of your income will be replaced by your retirement benefits. If your lifetime earnings were average, you can expect to receive a benefit of about $17,532 a year. An eligible couple with average earnings receives about $29,376 a year (both worker and spouse at full retirement age).

If you have always paid the maximum in Social Security deductions, you can count on a benefit of about 26% of that amount. In 2020, the maximum earnings subject to Social Security taxes are $137,700, generating approximately $35,800 a year in retirement benefits. As long as you work, you will pay FICA taxes.

Important Ages

As you look ahead to retirement, you may be thinking, "The earlier, the better." But if Social Security is going to be your main source of income, "the later, the better" applies.

If you choose to start receiving benefits when you reach full retirement age (FRA), you will receive your full benefit. Your FRA depends on what year you were born. **(See the chart on page 36.)**

If you start receiving benefits before FRA, as early as age 62, your benefits will be permanently reduced by up to 30%, depending on when your benefits start. If you delay receiving benefits after FRA, up to age 70, you can earn credits that increase your monthly benefit by about 8% for each year you delay. **Read more about early retirement or late retirement in Chapter 4.**

Early retirement decreases your retirement benefits. If you take your benefits before FRA,

A study by MassMutual of those who have filed Social Security retirement benefits found:

- 30% filed at age 62 or younger
- 38% wish they had filed later
- 53% filed for Social Security out of financial necessity, such as not saving enough
- 30% filed for Social Security because of unforeseen issues, such as health issues or employment changes.

as early as age 62, they are permanently reduced. The amount of the reduction depends on the number of months you elect benefits prior to FRA. **Note:** At FRA, even if you had previously filed for reduced benefits, you will be given credit for any months you did not receive a full check because of work. This is commonly referred to by Social Security as an automatic adjustment of your reduction factor.

If you decide to retire before FRA or you have very low earnings, you may want to consider filing early. **For a more detailed explanation of the best time to contact Social Security to avoid possible loss of benefits, refer to the section titled "When to Contact Social Security" on page 42.**

Other options used to be available at FRA. **For more information, visit www.ssa.gov/planners /retire/claiming.html.**

Estimated Monthly and First-Year Social Security Income Payable in 2020 to a Person Attaining Full Retirement Age (FRA)

Salary in Year Before Retirement (2019)	Monthly Social Security Income	First-Year Social Security Income	Percent of Salary Replaced by Social Security Benefit
$30,000	$1,194	$14,328	41%
$40,000	$1,407	$16,884	37%
$50,000	$1,620	$19,440	34%
$60,000	$1,832	$21,984	28%
$90,000	$2,437	$29,244	27%
$120,000	$2,736	$32,832	23%

Source: www.ssa.gov/OACT/quickcalc/index.html.
Benefit estimates made by the Social Security Quick Calculator are rough because it makes an assumption about earnings history.

Notes to chart: Except for people who have always paid the maximum, the amount payable in any particular case could vary greatly from these figures. In fact, people who spent much of their careers in jobs without Social Security coverage or outside the workforce altogether will likely receive less payment. These figures assume that the worker does not qualify for a noncovered pension. Anyone who does qualify for a pension based on work that was not covered for Social Security taxes may not have the same computation method.

These figures assume a worker attaining FRA in 2020 who earned the salaries shown in 2019, assuming steady work and yearly wage increases for 35 years prior to retirement.

Because $132,900 was the maximum taxable 2019 Social Security wage base, Social Security will replace an increasingly smaller portion of earnings that exceed it.

The maximum amount of earnings covered by Social Security was lower in past years than it is now. Those years of lower limits must be counted in with the higher ones of recent years to figure your average earnings and the amount of your monthly retirement benefit payment.

Maximum benefits for a worker attaining FRA in 2020 is $3,011 per month.

Spouses: Retirement Benefits

Today, in many families, both spouses have worked and paid Social Security taxes. However, both spouses are eligible to receive Social Security benefits even if only one has earned enough credits.

If only one spouse qualifies, at retirement, the worker who qualifies will receive his or her own benefits. The nonqualified spouse (the spouse who has not worked enough to qualify) will receive a benefit equal to a percentage of the worker's benefit. Usually, the nonqualified spouse must be age 62 to receive this spousal benefit.

If both spouses qualify on their own for Social Security, both will receive their own benefits. In those instances where one spouse's FRA benefit is less than half of the other's FRA amount, the lesser paid spouse will usually receive his or her own benefit *plus* a spousal benefit.

An eligible divorced spouse age 62 or over whose marriage lasted ten years or longer may be eligible for Social Security benefits based on the earnings of

Once you are on the Social Security rolls, your benefit payments will increase automatically but may not keep pace with increases in the cost of living.

In addition, additional earnings after initial entitlement can be considered in a recalculation of your rate.

an ex-spouse. If you qualify for your own benefits as well, you are usually allowed to receive the larger of either your benefit or your share of your ex-spouse's benefit. If you remarry, you generally cannot collect benefits on your ex-spouse's record unless your later marriage ends. **For more information, visit www.ssa.gov/planners/retire/divspouse.html.**

OTHER RESOURCES

Social Security Administration provides helpful pamphlets. Call (800) 772-1213 to request copies, or visit www.ssa.gov/pubs.

- *Windfall Elimination Provision*
- *If You Are a Farm Worker*
- *Government Pension Offset*
- *How Workers' Compensation and Other Disability Payments May Affect Your Benefits*
- *Household Workers*
- *How Work Affects Your Benefits*
- *Your Retirement Benefit: How It Is Figured*

- *Military Service and Social Security*
- *If You Are Self-Employed*
- *What You Need to Know: Reviewing Your Disability*
- *Your Right to Representation*
- *Special Payments After Retirement*
- *The Appeals Process*
- *When You Retire From Your Own Business: What You Need to Know*

The spousal benefit provisions in no way reduce the worker's benefits. Similarly, spousal benefits payable to a current spouse are not affected by any benefits being paid to a former spouse.

Survivor Benefits

Some of the Social Security taxes a worker pays are for survivor benefits when the worker dies. Survivor benefits can be paid to spouses, children and parents. (Refer to the chart on page 41 for more specific information.)

Survivor benefits can be paid based on fully or currently insured worker status.

Some survivor benefits can be paid if the worker is not fully insured but has earned credits in six of the 13 calendar quarters prior to death. By doing so, the worker is considered to be currently insured. This is especially helpful when young workers die, leaving dependent children and widows/ers caring for those children.

The amount of benefits payable to any survivor is determined by the covered earnings of the deceased worker. A rate is calculated as if the worker was age 62 in the year of death, and a PIA is established. Each dependent is entitled to a percentage of the PIA; however, there is a maximum amount payable to a family. Benefits

SOCIAL SECURITY PAYMENT DATES

New beneficiaries will have benefits directly deposited based on their day of birth:

1-10—Second Wednesday of the month

11-20—Third Wednesday of the month

21-31—Fourth Wednesday of the month

due to divorced spouses are not considered in the family maximum. In other words, the divorced spouse takes nothing away from the current spouse or widow and vice versa.

A one-time death payment of $255 is payable to either a widow/er entitled to benefits or a widow/er not entitled to monthly benefits or to children entitled to benefits.

Widows and Widowers

Social Security benefits will be continued for widows, surviving divorced spouses, and disabled widows and widowers who remarry. Widows with more than one prior spouse may have more than one choice of survivor benefits for Social Security.

The earliest a widow/er can start receiving Social Security survivor benefits based on age is at age 60.

Widow/er benefits based on age can start any time between age 60 and FRA as a survivor. Taking survivor benefits before FRA means the widow/er collects benefits for a longer period of time but the survivor benefits may be reduced for each month before full retirement age.

If a person receives widow/er benefits and will qualify for a retirement benefit that's more than their survivor benefit, they can switch to their own retirement benefit as early as age 62 or as late as age 70. The rules are complicated. Each widow/er's situation is different, and you should contact Social Security as soon as possible after the death of the worker.

Before you decide to switch, we recommend that you find out what the dollar amount of your own retirement benefits would be at 62, at FRA and at age 70. Most widows/ers are told the rates for age 62 and FRA; however, Social Security employees may fail to tell you what the rate would be if you wait until age 70. At age 70, delayed retirement credits can be added to your own basic retirement benefit and will significantly increase the total retirement benefit payment.

Social Security Benefits for Dependents

Dependent Is Age	And	Then These Benefits May Be Payable	At the Following Percentage of PIA***
0 to 19	A child of a deceased or entitled worker*	Minor child or student benefits	50% (worker alive) 75% (worker deceased)
18 and older	Disabled before age 22 and parent is either deceased or entitled	Disabled adult child benefits	50% (worker alive) 75% (worker deceased)
Up to FRA**	A young widow/er or divorced widow/er with child in care under age 16	Mother/father benefits	75%
50 to 60	A disabled widow/er or surviving divorced widow/er	Disabled widow/er benefits	71.5%
60+	A widow/er or surviving divorced spouse	Widows/ers benefit	Varies from 71.5% to 100%, depending on age at entitlement
62+	1. Currently married to entitled worker	Spouse benefits	Varies from 22.8% to 50%, depending on age at entitlement
	2. Divorced after ten years of marriage to entitled worker	Divorced spouse benefits	82.5%, if one; 75% each, if two
	3. Divorced after ten years of marriage to an age 62 worker not entitled but insured	Independently entitled divorced spouse benefits	
	4. Surviving parent(s)	Parent benefits	

There is a family maximum of benefits that can be paid on a worker's record. To keep within the family maximum, benefits for dependents may have to be adjusted.

*See Chapter 15 for information for grandchildren.   **Full retirement age   ***Primary insurance amount

There have been many widows/ers who were told that there was no need to file a claim on their own work because the survivors rate was higher. They were not advised that if they waited until age 70 to file on their own work record, their own retirement check amount would exceed the survivor rate. Widows/ers who are eligible on the records of more than one prior spouse need to examine their choices carefully.

Disability Benefits

The risk of disability hangs over all of us. A loss of earnings due to severe injury or illness can affect a family more than retirement or death.

Social Security provides basic protection against disability for those who meet its definition of covered workers and their families.

Waiting period. There is a five-month waiting period before disability payments can begin. The

When to Contact Social Security

- Survivors of deceased workers should contact Social Security as soon as possible after the death of the worker.

- Disabled workers should contact Social Security as soon as a physician advises that a medical condition is expected to last at least 12 months.

Everyone should:

- Contact Social Security three months prior to age 62 if you have retired or are planning to retire at age 62.

OR

- Contact Social Security every January (even if working full-time). Provide them with an estimate of your current year earnings, and ask them to determine the dollar amount of any benefits you might be eligible for if you filed a formal claim. Remember to tell Social Security if there are any dependents who will also be eligible for benefits on your record. In many cases, a worker is better off to file for benefits effective with January of the year they become FRA rather than effective with the month they become FRA.

AND

- Regardless of when you retire, be sure to contact Social Security three months prior to age 65 for Medicare benefits. Although FRA has increased, Medicare is still effective as of age 65.

waiting period begins with the first full month of disability and ends five months later. No payment is made for that period.

How to qualify. Disability benefits require the worker not only to be fully insured but also to have recent work.

Recent work means during the ten-year period just before becoming disabled, the worker must have five years of credits (20). Workers becoming disabled prior to age 31 need fewer credits. Workers who are statutorily blind must only be fully insured.

It is very important for a worker to understand the recent work requirement, particularly people opting for early retirements with their company. If you plan on retiring prior to age 56, you should consider working at another job and acquiring four credits per year through the year you attain age 56. By doing so, you will continue to have enough recent work to qualify for disability until you reach age 62.

Dependents of disabled workers can also receive benefits within the family maximum payable. There are no disabled spouse benefits.

Medicare Benefits

Medicare is a national health insurance program for people who are age 65, have been receiving Social Security disability benefits for 24 months, have end-stage renal disease or have become disabled due to ALS. Medicare is administered by the Social Security Administration. The Department of Health and Human Services is responsible for processing reimbursements for covered medical services.

Whether or not you apply for Social Security retirement benefits at age 65, you should apply for Medicare at least three months in advance of your 65th birthday to be covered by Medicare. If you enrolled in Social Security before you turned 65, you will automatically be enrolled in Medicare when you turn 65. **(See Chapter 8.)**

Work and Social Security

You can get Social Security retirement or survivor benefits and work at the same time. But if you're younger than FRA and earn more than certain amounts, your benefits will be reduced.

Social Security beneficiaries are subject to the earnings limit up until the month of FRA (see chart on page 36) except for a disabled worker or an adult disabled child. The earnings limit increases every year. Earnings include only income from work or from self-employment. Earnings do not include investment income (dividends, real estate, rentals and return on capital) and pensions.

If you are less than FRA throughout 2020, the earnings limit is $18,240. For people reaching FRA in 2020, the limit is $48,600; however, only earnings up to the month of FRA are counted.

If you earn more than the yearly limit, you will lose some of your Social Security benefits. One dollar is withheld for every two dollars above the limit for all persons younger than FRA throughout the year. One dollar in benefits will be deducted for each three dollars above the annual limit for persons attaining FRA during the year. This one-for-three rule is significant.

SOCIAL SECURITY: THEN AND NOW

When the Social Security Act was passed, the average American died at age 63. Most people wouldn't live to collect Social Security, and those who did wouldn't collect it for long.

Today, the average American will live to about 78 (76 for men and 81 for women).

When Social Security was launched in 1937, more than 40 contributors supported each recipient. A lot has changed since then. Longevity has increased. Social Security has expanded to include more benefits and more recipients. Starting in 1975 and through today, about three contributors support each recipient.

Many people could receive some Social Security benefits for months before FRA even while working full-time.

There is a special rule that can apply to your initial year of retirement. It is called the *grace year rule,* meaning that workers are allowed a monthly earning limit for each month in that year. The monthly limit is simply the annual limit divided by 12. This special rule usually applies only for one year but helps those persons who have high earnings in the months prior to retirement.

There is no earnings limit once you reach FRA. Earnings during the month you become FRA and thereafter do not count toward the annual limit. **For more information, visit www.ssa.gov /planners/retire/whileworking.html.**

Benefits May Be Taxable

Up to 85% of your benefits may be subject to the federal income tax for any year in which your adjusted gross income plus nontaxable interest income and one-half of your Social Security benefits exceed a base amount of $25,000 for an individual, $32,000 for a couple and zero for a couple filing separately. If you would like to have income taxes withheld from your check, contact Social Security.

Supplemental Security Income

People in financial need who are 65 or older or people of any age who are blind or disabled may be eligible for a monthly cash payment from the federal government. These payments are called supplemental security income (SSI).

People may be eligible for payments if they have little or no regular cash income and don't own much in the way of assets that can be turned into cash. The Social Security Administration operates the program, but SSI is not the same as Social Security. Social Security funds are not used to make SSI payments. Applications for SSI are made at the Social Security office. In most states, Medicaid is provided for anyone eligible for SSI.

Retire Early or Late

"You have to put off being young until you can retire." —Author Unknown

When Should You Retire?

This is fast becoming the No. 1 question on the minds of many workers.

American workers have wide-ranging choices to make when they try to pinpoint a retirement age. For many workers today, the time span is from 50 to 70—a 20-year time period. With greater freedom in selecting a date for retirement, it is important that you choose carefully. There are pros and cons to each option. Today, nearly four in ten workers say they want to retire before age 65, according to the Employee Benefit Research Institute (EBRI). In considering your options, remember that if you work even a few extra years, you can dramatically improve your retirement assets, particularly if your job has a retirement plan and health insurance.

The right choice will help to ensure a successful retirement.

Retiring Unexpectedly

For some workers, early retirement is not necessarily a free and happy choice. In planning, you should be prepared for the unforeseen. According to an EBRI survey, 50% of workers who planned to work longer had to retire unexpectedly due to a hardship such as a health problem or disability or because of changes at their companies. Only 14% of people stopped working at the age they predicted. Many people retire before 65 due to the loss of a job or family members in need of caretaking. A higher percentage of women retiring early cite such reasons.

Your Options

The federal Age Discrimination in Employment Act bars mandatory retirement except under a few circumstances. Older workers must be assessed for continued employment solely on a basis of ability—not age. If, based on your personal circumstances, the choice is up to you, then you have three options.

- You can retire and stop working at your full retirement age (FRA) and begin collecting Social Security (or not). **(See page 36.)**
- You can continue working and choose whether or not to claim Social Security benefits.
- You can take early retirement. This could mean before FRA as defined by Social Security or a retirement age defined by your employer's

plan. You may choose to begin collecting Social Security if you're eligible, or you may choose to delay claiming Social Security.

When to Retire

Current Social Security law gradually increases the FRA from 65 to 67 by the year 2027. **(See page 37 for a discussion of how your Social Security benefits will be affected by a decision to retire early.)**

The decision of when to retire—before, at or after FRA—ideally should depend on your personal circumstances. There are many things to consider. You may want to quit earlier, take your pension and find an easier job. You may want to work past 66 or 67 to meet continuing high costs for medical care, children's or parent's expenses, or other needs. Or you may be ready to quit at 66 or 67 to take life easier. Finances are not the only thing to think about. Retirement is a mental health consideration. Being emotionally grounded going into retirement will likely lead to better financial decisions.

Work satisfaction is another important factor in making decisions about whether to continue on the job as long as you can or to retire early. If you have a physical job and the work is getting too demanding, and particularly if doctors recommend taking things easier in your 50s or early 60s, retiring may be the right thing to do. However, most people are still physically fit and able to continue on the job beyond their FRA.

If you are part of a two-career couple, you should consider whether you want to retire at the same time. Separate retirement dates can offer

Your Retirement Finances

Experts say 80-130% of your preretirement income is needed to maintain living standards in retirement. The examples below show how much retirement income may be needed. While the estimated first year of Social Security income remains steady, the income needed from savings, investment and work goes up as the percentage of income needed goes up.

Percent of income needed to maintain living standards	80%	100%	130%	Your Numbers
Income from last year at work	40,000	40,000	40,000	
Retirement income	32,000	40,000	52,000	
Estimated first year of Social Security income at FRA	14,688	14,688	14,688	
Income needed from pension, investments, and full- or part-time work	17,312	25,312	37,312	

The above is for your first year of retirement. Taking the 80% example, ten years from now, with a 4% inflation rate, instead of $32,000, you'll need approximately $47,400. Social Security is indexed for inflation and, assuming it's not changed, will return approximately $21,742. You'll then need another $25,658 from your pension, work and investments to maintain your present living standard.

advantages, including extending employer health insurance to cover the retired spouse.

Do You Feel Ready to Retire?

Whatever you do, whenever you retire, remember that you face psychological changes. Retirement is a stage of life that stirs up intense feelings of excitement, liberation, fear and anxiety. Retirement for many involves a leap of faith after decades of routine. Retirement is a major transition that unfolds over many years, and the journey will require flexibility and resilience.

If regular work is such a habit for you that the very thought of breaking it by retiring is a psychological problem, then perhaps working beyond FRA is your answer. Idleness may give you a feeling of guilt, a loss of self-esteem or a feeling of withdrawal from society. But remember, in the long run, the substitution of new things—work and play and just plain relaxing—may be better for you.

In retirement, you must face yourself anew. Try to keep free of self-pity and bitterness. Accept your situation, compensate for whatever losses might come, and remind yourself that what is important is not what you've lost but what you still have and still can do.

In short, learn to focus on retirement as a positive experience. Retirement is a new beginning; it gives you the chance to develop and expand your interests in ways that were not possible during your working years. Before retirement, much of your time is taken up by the day-to-day necessity of work. In retirement, the end of that routine means the beginning of new opportunities.

Before You Decide

With the help of your employee benefits department at work and/or someone in the Social Security office, find out whether staying on the job beyond FRA would substantially increase your eventual retirement benefits. Find out when and in what form you can receive your benefits at retirement.

For some, particularly those who have been jobless over long periods or have changed jobs frequently so that years of service for one employer haven't accumulated sufficiently to fully vest, working beyond FRA is likely a step toward a more adequate income in retirement.

If you're thinking about retiring early, check with your Social Security office to find out how much you'll forfeit in benefits, and check with your company personnel office to find out how your pension will be affected. When it comes to Social Security, retiring at 62 could reduce your benefits by about 20% compared with working to FRA. **Try this calculator: www.ssa.gov/OACT/quickcalc /early_late.html**

Can You Afford to Retire?

Revisit your cash flow, debt management, and savings and investment program. Review your sources of income in retirement. People who are not covered by a pension plan may need to continue to work as long as possible.

Do you need to continue working for income and employee benefits?

For example, are you paying off a mortgage or other debts? If so, do you need to continue receiving a regular paycheck to do it comfortably?

Do you have some other important financial need that can best be met by continuing in your regular job beyond FRA? Under such circumstances, the ability to work can be a blessing.

Health care costs continue to escalate. Do you need health insurance through your employer? Do you qualify for Medicare? Even if you do, Medicare does not cover a number of health items that you'll have to pay for yourself. **(See Chapter 8.)**

Take into consideration that working a few more years can make the difference between enjoying a comfortable lifestyle or having difficulty paying bills. Even with the best-laid plans, circumstances can change your financial status. Plan for potential health problems, family issues and financial bumps in the road.

Early Retirement

Carefully consider the pros and cons of early retirement—the possible rewards and the potential pitfalls. Those who have worked for three or four decades may find inactivity difficult. Some people must substitute something else for work.

You should have a carefully thought-out new life ahead. While that is true for everyone who retires, regardless of their age, it is particularly true for those retiring early. Younger retirees must look ahead not for an average decade or two, as those 66 or 67 must, but for as long as three decades.

If you're going to start a new life early, ask yourself what it is going to be like. Early retirement is not for everyone. You should be ready for it and able to take it in full stride and enjoy it. Most of all, you must be able to afford it, not just at the time of early retirement but also through the years to come.

Those wondering whether they should retire early should consider the following:

- Why do I want to retire early? Retire early to what? Do I have a new life waiting for me? Do I have a new job waiting for me?
- If you are considering early retirement without plans to take another job, full- or part-time, what then?
- Are you really ready for all the leisure you'll have? Can you fill your time with community service, educational opportunities, hobbies, travel, sports, cards, etc.? It sounds easy to do, but the transition isn't easy for many retirees. **(See more questions on page 50.)**

Think about how many years you likely have ahead of you and make sure, by advance planning, that you can make them active and fulfilling years. If you are in your 50s and do not have a job waiting for you, be wary of retiring early unless you have sufficient reserves to make additional income unnecessary. The years you'll spend in retirement can be 15 to 30 years or more. Keep in mind that retiring earlier will decrease the amount of money you can safely withdraw.

Retire early if you can enjoy your later years free of financial worries and free of boredom. Stay on the job if you aren't sure you can.

Delayed Retirement

The reason today's retirees may stay working longer is primarily economics. They won't be as ready to retire at 55, or maybe even at 66 or 67, because of inadequate savings, reduced employer benefits and the possible scaling back of what the federal government will provide.

As the rules governing Social Security payments gradually change, with full benefits eventually not kicking in until age 67, people may find further incentives to keep working.

Even without such a change in the rules, though, many retiring workers could be in for a

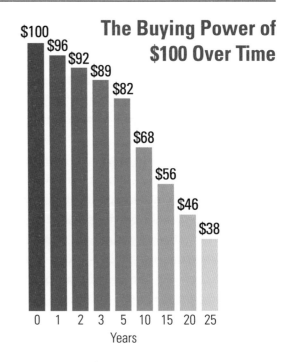

The Buying Power of $100 Over Time

$100 $96 $92 $89 $82 $68 $56 $46 $38

0 1 2 3 5 10 15 20 25
Years

The buying power of $100 decreases as the price of goods increases with inflation. This chart assumes a 4% annual average inflation rate. Social Security is indexed for inflation, but your pension may not be, so your investments should earn 4% after taxes to stay even.

shock at the size of their monthly Social Security benefit payments.

It is probably true that today's mature workers are better able to keep plugging away at a job. Many 60-year-olds are healthier than those a generation ago. Moreover, fewer jobs now require heavy physical labor. Reeducating and retraining older workers could prolong their work lives.

Consider this: The longer you work, the harder it may be to adjust to retirement. It may be easier to change your lifestyle when you are more active and healthy than in your later years. You will likely adapt more readily to the things you would enjoy doing but haven't had an opportunity to do, and it will be easier to slip into a new, less arduous job if you want to supplement your retirement pay.

Inflation

Every retiree should be aware of the impact of inflation because it is a problem that is likely to continue. Even when the rate of inflation is fairly low, it still remains a factor. A 4% annual rate of inflation amounts to a rise of more than 20% in the cost of living in just five years.

Remember, dollars are worth less year to year. It can be difficult to live with inflation while you're working, and it will be even harder when you retire on a fixed income. Costs go up and, even with cost-of-living changes in Social Security benefits, the income of retirees may not keep up with living costs.

The problems will be considerably worse for those who elect to retire earlier with smaller pensions and Social Security payments. Assess how the changes in the economy will affect your pension, investments and retirement benefits.

Unless you can retire early and build up your reserves through a new job, a new business or a new career, you will probably be better off economically working longer and concentrating on accumulating savings for a more secure future.

Inflation will reduce the value of your retirement dollars. Social Security is indexed for inflation, but

IMPORTANT AGES

- **55:** If you retire at this age, you can take penalty-free 401(k) withdrawals from your account with your most recent employer. If you have a pension plan, some plans allow reduced pension payments as early as age 55.

- **59½:** The 10% early withdrawal penalty on IRA withdrawals no longer applies.

- **62:** You can begin collecting reduced Social Security retirement benefits.

- **65:** You're eligible for Medicare.

- **66-67:** You can begin collecting unreduced Social Security at your FRA depending on the year you were born.

- **70:** You can increase your Social Security payments if you delay claiming your benefit until age 70. After age 70, there is no added benefit to delaying Social Security.

- **70½:** You're required to take annual withdrawals from 401(k) plans and traditional IRAs and pay the resulting income tax. Your first distribution must be taken by April 1 of the year after you turn 70½.

the index doesn't fully cover the increased costs of medical care and goods and services.

Your pension may be indexed, but many are not.

Your investments should earn the rate of inflation plus taxes for you to stay even financially.

Retire to a Second Career

Do you need to bring in additional income? Do you seek personally fulfilling work? Do you have a job waiting for you? Ideally, you will want to plan your second career while you are still working.

Early Retirement

Detailed planning for retirement should begin five to ten years before you retire. If you are thinking about early retirement, consider the following questions.

- Do you have something definite you want to do after early retirement? Is there something you have always wanted to do that you can undertake in your late 50s or early 60s? A second, deeply satisfying career, perhaps?

- Is your pension or savings enough to bridge the gap between your early retirement and the time you'll start receiving Social Security payments?

- Have you factored in inflation? If inflation averages 4%, $1,000 in today's money will be worth $375 in 25 years.

- Have you planned sufficiently for early retirement with your spouse and other members of your family?

- Are major debts paid off or under control?

- How will you maintain health insurance between the time you leave your job and group plans and when you will become eligible for Medicare?

- Have you planned for unexpected developments like becoming widowed or divorced, developing health problems or taking care of ailing parents?

- Have you talked to other early retirees? How are they doing? If people you know are living the retirement life you want, have you learned how they got it?

- Are you sure that early retirement is what you really want? Will it make you happier? If you are married and have kids, will it make your spouse and family happier?

According to EBRI, 80% of workers plan to work in retirement; however, workers are far more likely to plan to work in retirement than retirees are to have actually worked.

Remember, if you are considering retirement, it's easy to talk casually about resting up for a while and then getting a new job. But those who do not have highly marketable skills could run into difficulty in finding a new position. You might find that it's awfully hard to find a new job once you have left the workforce. (**See Chapter 10 for ideas about earning money.**)

It can help to keep your skills current or develop new ones by, for example, taking a class. (**See Chapter 13 for more ideas about keeping up to date.**)

Retirement vs. Vacation

Many people plan their vacations with more detail than their retirement. But deciding to retire without planning can put a successful transition and a satisfying retirement at risk. Start your planning early—at least five years before your planned date.

Checklist for
Before You Retire

When your retirement is approaching, here are some things you should do.

Yes No

○ ○   Most important, make realistic plans for day-to-day living in retirement. Review estimates of what your financial needs will be for living costs, housing, insurance, health care, transportation, utilities, clothing, recreation and miscellaneous costs. If inflation changes, earlier cost-of-living estimates may no longer be accurate. Review estimates of income sources.

○ ○   Begin developing retirement interests and activities. If you are married, these considerations should be both individual and joint.

○ ○   Get your papers in order, especially the documents you will need to claim Social Security benefits: Social Security cards; proof of age, preferably a birth certificate; and your marriage license, if married.

○ ○   Register with your Social Security office about three months in advance of your retirement in order to receive your first payment in the month after you retire. It takes that long to process applications. If married, your spouse should go with you. Take the documents you need, including a copy of your last two W-2 tax forms, withholding statements and your spouse's tax papers if both of you are working.

○ ○   Check with former employers to find out whether you might be due partial pensions based on their contributions to pension plans on your behalf when you were employed. Vesting rules vary. Some retirees lose money because they neglect to check with former employers about pensions. (See Chapter 2.)

○ ○   If you have a pension, decide on your options. Ask the employee benefits department of your company to work out the details of your pension. Ask how and when pension checks will arrive. Find out if you're restricted from working full- or part-time once you start receiving your pension. If you are married, you need to decide between monthly payments that end with your life or continue on to a surviving spouse. (See Chapter 14.)

Yes No

○   ○   Decide on how you will draw down your 401(k), IRA and other retirement income accounts.

○   ○   Decide on options for handling your mortgage or other financial obligations that will continue after retirement.

○   ○   Decide on whether cars and appliances should be replaced while your income is at its maximum. It's generally a good idea to replace appliances that are more than ten years old. Also consider your basic clothing needs.

○   ○   Have a medical checkup while you are still covered by your company's medical program. It will save you money.

○   ○   Decide on health insurance needs. (See Chapter 8.)

○   ○   Under some conditions, retirement benefits are available to war veterans with limited incomes or to widows of veterans. To qualify, veterans must be permanently or totally disabled due to a service or nonservice injury. If you think you might qualify, check with your nearest Veterans Affairs office.

○   ○   Check with your employee benefits department on your options for accrued vacation or sick leave time (often you can get a lump-sum payment), whether life insurance carries over or must be switched from a group plan to an individual policy, and whether health insurance can be continued.

○   ○   Visualize the kind of person you want to become in retirement, share your vision with other people and get their feedback—especially people who have successfully made the transition to retirement.

In a nutshell, when you retire, be ready. Know what retirement will mean and how you will acclimate to it.

Checklist for
When You Retire

So, you've retired. What now?

Your advance planning should have given you an answer to that question. Review how things are going compared with what you planned for. Here are some more items you should consider.

Yes No

○ ○   If you have received a lump-sum payment from a qualified pension or defined contribution plan, talk to someone at your bank or a reputable brokerage about how it can be best used to meet your future needs. Don't consider the big check a windfall and go on a spending spree. Remember, it's taxable money.

○ ○   You may avoid an immediate tax on a lump-sum payment by having your employer transfer the money directly to an IRA within 60 days. (See page 27.)

○ ○   If you have any long-term savings or tax-deferred investments, check with your banker or broker about the advisability of changes to these accounts. (See Chapter 2.)

○ ○   Your tax position changes with retirement. Social Security benefits are taxable if your adjusted gross income plus nontaxable interest and half of your Social Security benefit are more than a base amount (the base for an individual is $25,000; for a couple filing jointly, it is $32,000), but part or all of your pension and retirement/ investment accounts will be subject to income taxes. So will income you may have from part-time or other work and from most other sources. Unless you take another regular job, you won't have money withheld to cover continuing taxes. Be prepared to handle more tax work—and tax payments on your own. If you have any questions, call or email the Internal Revenue Service for answers.

○ ○   Consider ways to cut insurance costs. Does your auto insurer offer a premium rate to drivers of retirement age who do not use cars to drive to work? Some do. If your car is more than four years old, check with your agent about dropping the collision insurance in your policy; it might not be worth the cost. And if you plan to buy a new car, check on insurance rates for the cars you're interested in: Rates differ from model to model.

○ ○   Reassess the adequacy of your home insurance every year. With inflation, repair and replacement costs are rising year to year. Be sure you are sufficiently protected against losses from fire or other hazards.

○ ○   Check with your life insurance agent as to whether you can convert your present coverage to a paid-up policy and save on further premiums. You may not need the policy.

Yes No

◯ ◯   If you want to work, there are agencies in most counties or cities that help older workers find part-time or full-time employment. Any local agency that works with older people can refer you to one. You may also register with an employment agency. (See Chapter 10.)

◯ ◯   If you don't want a job but want to keep busy, investigate local volunteer service opportunities. Volunteers are in short supply everywhere. (See Chapter 12.)

◯ ◯   Check into recreation, education, community service and/or civic activities that offer enough in the way of new opportunities to provide a sound basis for a new life in retirement.

◯ ◯   Don't try to adapt overnight to your new life and your changed circumstances. Go at it slowly and carefully, remembering that retirement is not an end but a beginning.

Estate Planning

"Do not try to live forever. You will not succeed."

—George Bernard Shaw

What Will Happen in the Event of Your Death?

This chapter will provide information on wills, health care wishes and funeral arrangements to help you make future plans for your finances and property. Estate planning will help ensure that your wishes will be carried out in the event of your death and that your estate will be disposed of according to your plans. Making these plans can be done at any age and, in fact, is recommended for all adults in the event of an unexpected death.

What Is an Estate?

Before skipping to the next chapter, thinking that you don't have an estate and that everything will be left to your spouse, let's define an *estate*. An estate consists of everything you own: life insurance, accounts in banks and credit unions, Social Security, stocks, pension, real estate, furniture, cars, business and professional interests, investments, health savings accounts, etc.

Estate Taxes

At the federal level, only large estates are subject to estate taxes. Under current law, for the years 2018-2025, up to $11.18 million (adjusted annually for inflation) of an estate is exempt from federal taxation.

In 2020, when adjusted for inflation, the federal estate tax rate is 40% for those estates worth more than $11.58 million. Check these amounts regularly, since federal tax laws may change. Consult with an estate attorney to see how taxes will affect your estate. Some states have estate and/or inheritance taxes.

For the purpose of taxation:
- *Gross estate* is composed of all assets and property owned at the time of death and gifts made in contemplation of death.
- *Taxable estate* is the gross estate less liabilities.

Note: You can gift up to $15,000 a year (or $30,000 per couple) during your lifetime without incurring a gift tax.

DIGITAL ASSETS

Who will be able to access your online accounts after you die? Digital assets might be easily overlooked by the administrator of your estate if they don't know what accounts exist. Create a written list of your online accounts, including:

- Bank, investment and insurance accounts that do not mail printed statements to you
- Social media accounts
- Payment sites like PayPal
- Storage of digital photos, e-books, music, etc.
- Subscription accounts like video streaming or food delivery services
- Frequent flyer and other loyalty accounts
- Any bills you pay online like utility, phone and internet.

Keep the list updated, store it in a safe place, and let a trusted family member and your estate administrator know where the list is located.

You may wish to include passwords (except for high-value financial accounts like your bank account). The risk that your passwords might be stolen could be less serious than someone not being able to find them in an emergency.

Do not include passwords in your will because your will becomes part of the public record when it is filed for probate. Rather, add a line to your will explaining what you want done with your digital assets. For example, you may want certain accounts closed, or specify that the executor of your will can access your digital accounts.

Make a Will

A *will* is a written legal document that coordinates the disposition of your property after death. You name the person you wish to handle your estate and carry out the instructions in your will, called the *executor*. The executor can liquidate your assets, pay your taxes and debts, and disburse property to your heirs.

Your property will go to the person(s) named and in the amounts you specify in your will.

When You Don't Have a Will

Not having a will can result in disaster for your loved ones. Your assets may be divided according to state law and not your wishes. Without a will, you can leave your family dangerously vulnerable, with the court deciding who will raise your minor children.

If you are married, don't assume that your spouse will automatically receive your property. Even if you have all your property jointly owned, the absence of a will may cause your spouse to wait several months before gaining possession of the property.

Without a will:

- Your heirs will not be able to sell, distribute or handle property without the expense of asking a court for authority.
- Your estate or inheritance taxes may be higher than they need legally be, and the person who administers your estate will have to post a bond, the premium for which must be taken from the estate.
- Your property may be dealt with in ways that would go against your personal wishes.
- Your business may be operated or concluded.
- Your real estate may be sold with losses.

Where no will exists, the matter of who will administer the estate can be the occasion for painful disputes and needless expense.

Keeping Wills Up to Date

Wills should be reviewed every three to five years. Circumstances may have changed such that particulars referred to in the will no longer exist or things exist that the original will did not cover.

The following changes should cause you to look again at the condition of your will.

- Change of mind about beneficiaries or charities (Note: Beneficiary designations in your retirement account(s) and life insurance policy take precedence over anything you have in your will, so make the change to the account as well.)
- Death of executor
- Change in family situation
- Change in financial situation
- Change in the nature of assets
- Change in the needs of the beneficiaries
- Change of residence, state or country

Probate

A will provides your instructions. *Probate* with a will is a court-supervised procedure to validate and authenticate a will. The court officially appoints the executor named in the will, and the executor has the legal power to act on behalf of the deceased. Probate also refers to administering the estate of a deceased person without a will. The process varies from state to state.

Consider Trusts

Trusts may be an ideal method to handle some of your assets. A trust can be a valuable estate-planning tool if it will bypass probate. Trusts have advantages under certain conditions and could save money and time. Consult your attorney and accountant.

If you have a child with special needs, your estate plan can ensure that care for your child continues after your death. Consider hiring an attorney to create a special needs trust to set aside money specifically for special needs care rather than leaving money directly to the dependent or another family member. A special needs trust can hold money without the risk that your child would lose eligibility for Social Security Supplemental Security Income, Medicaid or state financial-need-based programs due to receiving an inheritance. Achieving a Better Life Experience (ABLE) accounts are another option to save money for disability-related expenses without losing eligibility for government programs. In addition to helping with trusts, special needs attorneys may be able

TYPES OF TRUSTS

You can create a trust by transferring your estate, or part of it, to a trustee who will hold your assets on behalf of your heir(s). Trusts can be arranged in many ways. Choose carefully.

- **Living trust:** With a living trust, also called a revocable trust, assets remain accessible to you during your lifetime. This trust designates to whom the remaining assets will be passed. You can name yourself trustee and also name a successor trustee to control assets upon your death. You also can have a fiduciary trustee manage the trust upon establishing it according to a written agreement. You can change or dissolve the trust.

- **Testamentary trust:** A testamentary trust is outlined in a will and created after your death, assuring income for your spouse or dependents and protecting them against their own inexperience in the management of the estate. It's subject to probate.

- **Irrevocable trust:** An irrevocable trust transfers your assets out of your estate, potentially reducing estate taxes. You lose control over the assets and cannot make changes or dissolve the trust.

to advise on considerations for your will and life insurance. **For a directory of attorneys, visit www.specialneedsalliance.org.**

Power of Attorney

Power of attorney allows someone to act as your agent while you are alive. Do not give away any more control than you absolutely have to. You can revoke your power of attorney at any time as long as you are mentally capable. This power can be broad or very specific and can include details such as handling your checking account, filing taxes or selling/buying a house.

A general power of attorney will cover all your day-to-day financial and personal decisions, while a limited power of attorney allows the agent to handle only specific matters, usually when you are unavailable or unable to do so. You should designate the scope of the responsibilities and/or the time period during which your agent can act for you.

If you become incapacitated, these powers will cease and you will need a durable power of attorney. A durable power of attorney names someone, typically a spouse, to make financial decisions for you when you are medically disabled.

Health Care Wishes

An *advance directive* is a legal document that explains how you want medical decisions to be made if you cannot make the decisions yourself or who you want to make those decisions. Advance directives only apply to health care decisions. The laws around advance directives are different from state to state. Talk to your health care provider, lawyer or local office on aging about filling out your advance directive while you are still healthy. All family members over the age of 18 should have one.

The most common types of advance directives are a living will and a durable power of attorney for health care.

A *living will* states your wishes to health care providers as to what artificial life-sustaining

procedures you want in the event of a terminal illness. Despite the name, it is not part of your will.

Durable power of attorney for health care, also known as a *medical power of attorney* or *health care proxy,* states your wishes about your future medical care. It tells health care providers whether you want to be kept alive if you're in a coma or suffering a terminal illness. It names someone you trust (an agent) to carry out your wishes. You should name a second person in the event the first is not available. It is important to communicate your desires with your agent in advance and have them agree to fulfill your wishes.

If you have a health savings account (HSA), there are some estate planning considerations. If you are married, designating your spouse as the beneficiary will maintain the account's tax-free status upon your death. If you are single or designate someone other than your spouse, the beneficiary will be taxed on the fair market value of the account.

Planning a Funeral

It is never easy to plan for a funeral, but planning in advance can make the process easier for your loved ones. Shop around for the best price, compare costs for the entire package, get a price list in writing and resist emotional overspending. A casket is often the most expensive item you'll buy. Put your preferences in writing (e.g., burial vs. cremation), and keep your plan in a safe place. Let a family member and your estate executor know where you keep it. Specify which charity or fund you would prefer as the recipient of memorial gifts.

Do not prepay your funeral expenses. Buying a small insurance policy or establishing a savings account to cover expenses will give you flexibility if you move, the firm goes out of business or you want to cancel the contract. **Consult the Funeral Consumers Alliance at (802) 865-8300 or www .funerals.org.**

If you served in the military, you could be eligible for burial benefits. **Contact Veterans Affairs at (800) 827-1000 or www.cem.va.gov.**

Where to Store What?

Safe deposit box: Use this option to store hard-to-replace items that you rarely need. Remember that items in safe deposit boxes will be accessible only during bank hours. Also, upon your death, access to the box may be caught up in the probate process. Items for a safe deposit box might include:

- Social Security card
- Birth, marriage, divorce and death certificates
- Paper stock and bond certificates
- Irreplaceable personal documents
- Family photos with sentimental value
- Collectibles (stamps, coins, baseball cards)
- Jewelry (inherited or special occasion; if you wear certain jewelry regularly, keep it at home in a safe.)
- Inventory of items in your home for insurance claims if disaster strikes
- Property records
- Car titles.

Safe place at home: Use this option to store items you or a loved one may need to access immediately. How and where to store these items in your home depends on your personal circumstances.

- Safe deposit box keys
- Jewelry you wear regularly
- Passport
- Spare keys (home, car)
- Funeral arrangements
- How you want personal items distributed
- CD or hard drive of digital photos
- List of digital/online accounts
- List of medications and contact info for your doctors and pharmacies
- Health care advance directives
- Power of attorney.

Estate Planning Resources

- FAQs on estate planning **www.americanbar.org/groups/real_property_trust_estate/resources/estate_planning**
- Health care advance planning **www.ambar.org/agingtoolkit**
- Five Wishes is a nationally used, popular advance directive template **www.fivewishes.org**
- CaringInfo, a program of the National Hospice and Palliative Care Organization **www.nhpco.org/patients-and-caregivers**
- National Institute on Aging **www.nia.nih.gov/health/caregiving/advance-care-planning**

Checklist for
Estate Planning

When you are planning for what will happen in the event of your death, here are some things you should do.

Yes No

○ ○ Review your finances, assets and debts with your spouse and family.

○ ○ Prepare written lists and instructions that include:

  – Will Fact Sheet (See page 61.)

  – Funeral/burial arrangements

  – Digital assets, passwords and PIN information

  – How to handle your personal possessions.

○ ○ Prepare a will with an estate lawyer, and review it periodically. Tell a trusted person where it is.

○ ○ Review current beneficiary designations on items such as your IRA, insurance policies, investments, annuities and company benefit plans. Don't leave any designations blank, because these will take precedence over anything in your will.

○ ○ Consider creating a living trust.

○ ○ Prepare a power of attorney for financial decisions.

○ ○ Prepare advance directives for health care.

○ ○ Tell a trusted person where your important records and instructions are stored.

If you receive an inheritance, protect your newfound wealth. Visit a financial planner to make a plan. Don't make hasty decisions.

Will Fact Sheet

Name: _____ Date this form was completed: _____

Cell phone: _____ Work phone: _____ Home phone: _____

Street address: _____

City: _____ County: _____ State: _____ ZIP code: _____

	Yourself	*Your Spouse*
Name:	_____	_____
Social Security number:	_____	_____
Occupation:	_____	_____
Date and place of birth:	_____	_____
Driver's license number:	_____	_____
Military service:	_____	_____

Date/place of marriage: _____ Date of divorce: _____

Death of spouse: _____

Children

Name: _____ Date and place of birth: _____

Cell phone: _____ Work phone: _____ Home phone: _____

Street address: _____

City: _____ County: _____ State: _____ ZIP code: _____

Spouse: _____

. . . .

Name: _____ Date and place of birth: _____

Cell phone: _____ Work phone: _____ Home phone: _____

Street address: _____

City: _____ County: _____ State: _____ ZIP code: _____

Spouse: _____

. . . .

Name: _____ Date and place of birth: _____

Cell phone: _____ Work phone: _____ Home phone: _____

Street address: _____

City: _____ County: _____ State: _____ ZIP code: _____

Spouse: _____

Benefit Plans

Pension plan: _____ Value (if known): $ _____

401(k) plan: _____ Value (if known): $ _____

Profit-sharing plan: _____ Value (if known): $ _____

Other: _____ Value (if known): $ _____

Other: _____ Value (if known): $ _____

Other: _____ Value (if known): $ _____

Other: _____ Value (if known): $ _____

Other: _____ Value (if known): $ _____

Health Insurance

Company: _____ Policy number: _____

Street address: _____ Agent: _____

City/state/ZIP code: _____ Beneficiaries: _____

Phone: _____ Location of policy: _____

Company: _____ Policy number: _____

Street address: _____ Agent: _____

City/state/ZIP code: _____ Beneficiaries: _____

Phone: _____ Location of policy: _____

Home and Auto Insurance

Company: _____ Policy number: _____

Street address: _____ Agent: _____

City/state/ZIP code: _____ Type of coverage: _____

Phone: _____ Location of policy: _____

Company: _____ Policy number: _____

Street address: _____ Agent: _____

City/state/ZIP code: _____ Type of coverage: _____

Phone: _____ Location of policy: _____

Assets Inventory

	Current Value	Original Cost	Ownership	Location
Home:				
Business:				
Savings account:				
Checking account:				
Pension plans:				
Household furniture:				
Collections:				
Bonds:				
Trust funds:				
Stocks:				
Other:				

Liability Inventory

Loans: _____ Amount: $ _____

Debts: _____ Amount: $ _____

Mortgages: _____ Amount: $ _____

Other: _____ Amount: $ _____

Life Insurance

Company/agent: _____ Face amount of policy: $ _____

Type of policy: _____ Cash surrender value: $ _____

Policy number: _____ Accidental death provision: _____

Phone: _____ Beneficiaries: _____

Company/agent: _____ Face amount of policy: $ _____

Type of policy: _____ Cash surrender value: $ _____

Policy number: _____ Accidental death provision: _____

Phone: _____ Beneficiaries: _____

Location of Records, Licenses, Etc.

Birth:_____

Marriage: _____

Adoption:_____

Citizenship: _____

Pre/postnuptial: _____

Divorce:_____

Discharge papers:_____

Building costs: _____

Deed:_____

Mortgage: _____

Title policy insurance: _____

Title abstract: _____

Surveys:_____

Insurance policies: _____

Tax receipts: _____

Leases: _____

Safe Deposit Box

Institution where located: _____

Street address:_____

City/state/ZIP code: _____

Contents:_____
_____

Box number: _____

Who has access:_____

Location of key: _____

People My Loved Ones May Need to Contact

Attorney: _____

Power of attorney: _____

Accountant: _____

Broker: _____

Doctor: _____

Banker: _____

Religious leader: _____

Employer: _____

Insurance agent:_____

Executor of estate: _____

Phone: _____

Phone: _____

Phone: _____

Phone: _____

Phone: _____

Phone: _____

Phone: _____

Phone: _____

Phone: _____

Phone: _____

Consumer Education

"People don't buy for logical reasons. They buy for emotional reasons."

—Zig Ziglar

Hanging on to Your Money

Hanging on to your retirement money can be a difficult task. It's important to keep your eyes wide open to avoid the common pitfalls that threaten to deplete your pocketbook. Following are some tips on being a better consumer and avoiding scams.

Cash, Credit or Debit?

Certain forms of payment are more psychologically painful than others. Security level varies too. What you decide to use is a personal decision and may depend on what you are buying.

Cash. Using cash allows you to feel the pain of actually being separated from the money you earn. You physically have the money and, when it's gone, it's really gone. Studies show that the more psychological pain we feel when we purchase something, the less likely we are to enjoy it or buy it at all. If cash is your main way to pay, you'll want to use a bank that has a wide network of ATMs or that reimburses fees for out-of-network ATM withdrawals in order to avoid fees. Cash has pros and cons as far as security goes. Cash is not subject to data breaches but, if you lose cash, you will probably never see it again.

Credit. Credit card rewards can be great for disciplined people who pay off their balance on time every month. But credit cards make it easy to overspend. Paying with a credit card can seem painless because there is a break in time between when you consume your purchase and when you have to pay for it. In your mind, the emotion you feel from the purchased item may not be linked to paying for it.

Here's one thing you can do to avoid overspending. Write down credit card purchases at the end of each day, either on a spreadsheet, in a budgeting app, or with a pen and paper. Instead of seeing the payment later on your statement, you will be confronting the purchase pain immediately, which may train you to treat your credit purchases as you would cash purchases.

Many credit card companies use fraud alerts to try to minimize the risk of credit card fraud. Federal law limits your maximum liability for unauthorized use of your credit card to $50, provided you notify the card company within 60 days. **(For tips on eliminating credit card debt, see Chapter 2.)**

Debit. Using a debit card protects you from potential credit card interest. But legally, debit cards have less protection from fraud than credit cards. You must report the debit card loss or theft to your bank within two business days to limit your loss to $50; after two days, it is raised to $500. After 60 days, there is no limit to your loss. Some banks allow more time, and some states have debit card laws. Reconcile your checking account regularly to watch for fraudulent purchases, and check your balance. If you have no overdraft protection, you may be able to avoid high overdraft fees for spending more than you have in your checking account because the merchant will decline your card.

Mobile payments. Cash may be your first choice to pay the babysitter or reimburse a friend for picking up the tab at lunch, and you may think to send a check to your brother in another state for his birthday. But peer-to-peer payment apps, such as Square Cash, PayPal and Venmo, may be faster and more convenient than using cash or check. Typically, you need the email address or phone number of the person you're sending money to, and he or she must be comfortable sharing account information with the app. The services usually have fees for using debit or credit to move money, but bank account transfers are free. Security risks include losing your phone, making your information vulnerable by using unsecured public Wi-Fi networks and having your passwords stolen.

Saving at the Grocery Store

People spend a significant percentage of their income on food. With these expenses come opportunities to save, including the following tips to cut costs on groceries.

- Always plan your food shopping. Make and use a list to avoid impulse buying. Bring a pen to the store, or use your smartphone, and track the price of each item you're picking up from your list. Add up your list before checking out to see if you're on track with your budget.
- Never shop while hungry.
- Shop only once or twice a week.

- Don't buy an item just because it's on sale. Look around on the shelf to compare prices.
- Consider buying store-brand items.
- Learn to compare cost per unit/price. Buying the larger size may not save you money.
- See if your local store offers a discount card for extra savings.

Unclaimed Funds

Billions of unpaid dollars are being held in state unclaimed fund accounts due to death, moving or closed accounts. **Start at www.usa.gov/unclaimed -money or contact your state controller or treasurer.** It's free for you to find and collect your money. Scammers may try to get you to pay a fee for this service—Do not pay.

Insurance

Picking insurance policies can be confusing—for any of the wide variety of insurance coverages. Policies differ, and what sounds similar may have features that change the premium.

Even two identical policies can vary considerably in cost from one insurer to another. Before you purchase, make sure you are dealing with a reputable company and compare its premium with those of competitors. **To help you evaluate premium expenses, check www.AccuQuote.com.**

Telemarketing

Chances are you've been called by telemarketers, often at inconvenient times and with a sales pitch for products and contests that don't interest you. Some may be fraudulent. Know your telemarketing rights. The Federal Trade Commission (FTC) created the National Do Not Call Registry. Registration is free, and most telemarketers cannot call your telephone number if it is in the National Do Not Call Registry. **To register, call (888) 382-1222 (you must call from the number you wish to register) or visit www.donotcall.gov.**

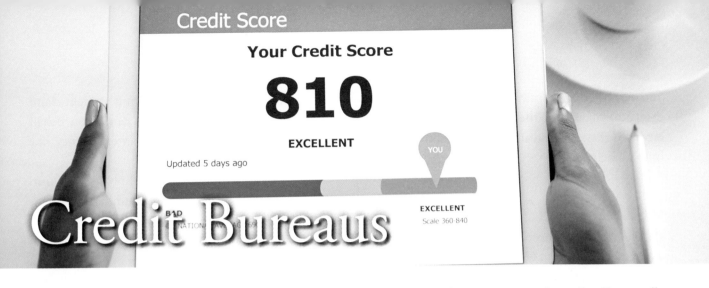

Credit Bureaus

Credit bureaus collect and store individual credit information and sell it to lenders, creditors and consumers in the form of a credit report.

Credit Reports

Review your credit report annually to protect yourself from identity theft. The Consumer Financial Protection Bureau recommends checking that the report contains only items about you. Be sure to look for information that is inaccurate or incomplete. If you find errors, contact the credit reporting company that sent you the report and the creditor or company that provided the information.

To request your free annual credit report, go to www.annualcreditreport.com or call (877) 322-8228. This report does not include your credit score, which can be ordered for a fee.

Prescreened Credit Offers

For every prescreened credit offer you receive, there will be inquiries on your credit report showing which companies obtained your information for prescreening, but those inquiries will not have a negative effect on your credit report or credit score. Cut up or shred prescreened credit offers that you will not use.

For more detail, visit www.consumer.ftc .gov/articles/0148-prescreened-credit-and -insurance-offers.

Stopping Credit Offers

The main reason people want to stop receiving prescreened offers is to make it less likely that a thief will intercept the offer and take out credit in their name.

To stop receiving prescreened credit offers, call (888) 5-OPTOUT or go to www.optoutprescreen .com. This website is the only one authorized by the nationwide credit bureaus. Through this website, you may request to opt out, meaning to remove your name from the mailing lists of each of the major nationwide credit bureaus, for five years. If you wish to permanently opt out, the website has a form to download, print and mail in. Opt Out Prescreen will not reach out to consumers, so any phone call or email from anyone claiming to be from Opt Out Prescreen is fraudulent.

Freezing Credit

If you are concerned about being the victim of identity theft, putting a freeze on your credit will make it very difficult for anyone but you to take out credit in your name. If you want to freeze your credit, you need to do it at each of the three major credit bureaus. It is free.

- Equifax: (800) 349-9960 or www.equifax.com
- Experian: (888) 397-3742 or www.experian.com
- TransUnion: (800) 909-8872 or www.transunion.com

Fraud Alerts

Putting a fraud alert on your credit is another option. Lenders will be notified to take extra steps to verify your identity before extending credit. Contact one credit bureau. The credit bureau you contact will then contact the other two. If you wish to call Equifax or TransUnion, the phone numbers for fraud alert are different than the numbers previously listed for freezing credit. Their numbers for fraud alert are:

- Equifax: (800) 525-6285
- TransUnion: (800) 680-7289.

You may still receive unwanted calls from robocallers that do not respect the registry. Robocalls use a recorded message instead of a live person. Hang up immediately.

Stop the Phone Scams

People over age 60 account for about 30% of fraud victims, according to Consumer Action. Everyone, no matter what age, is vulnerable to fraud. A phone scammer's goal is to get you to either send money or provide your personal information. Among the most common scams are phone calls from someone claiming to be from the government (IRS or Social Security) and asking for credit card or bank information, investment firms offering deals that require immediate payment, and people claiming to be calling on behalf of grandchildren or other relatives who are in trouble. The following are tips to spot and avoid phone scams.

- A phone number that appears to be local (using the same area code and first three digits of your number) may be a robocaller.
- Sham charities may call with high-pressure pitches for donations. Sadly, some claim to be charities that help wounded veterans or families of fallen police officers. Be skeptical of anyone who calls for the purpose of getting money from you for any reason.
- Take your time. Ask for written information about the subject of the call.
- If you don't want the seller to call you back, say so; if they call back, hang up. They're breaking the law.
- Don't make a decision on the call. Resist high-pressure sales tactics. Legitimate businesses respect that you're not interested. Before you respond to a phone solicitation about investments, talk to a friend, family member or financial advisor.
- Don't pay for prizes. Free is free!
- Don't send cash, gift cards, check or money order by courier or overnight delivery, and don't wire money to anyone who insists on immediate

payment. Be aware that a scammer might claim to be your relative, someone calling on behalf of a relative or experiencing an emergency like a kidnapping.

- Never give your credit card, bank account, Medicare or Social Security number to a caller.
- If you have been victimized once, be wary of callers offering to help you recover your losses for a fee paid in advance.

Suspect a scam? Contact your state attorney general.

Romance Scams

Scammers can target older people on online dating sites and social media platforms. Once a connection is established, the scammer often moves the communication off of the site to email and/or chat apps. Romance scammers ask for money while someone genuinely interested typically would not. Other common scams involve a love interest who lives in another country, is a deployed military servicemember or who always cancels scheduled in-person meetings. Don't send cash, wired money or gift cards. Victims of these scams can lose tens of thousands of dollars.

Internet Fraud

Treat all information that you receive on the internet, by email or by text message as you would any unsolicited information. Imposter scams account for 13% of consumer complaints to the Federal Trade Commission.

Phishing is when you get emails and texts that mimic the look of a legitimate company. Phishing messages typically ask people to provide usernames and passwords, credit and debit card numbers, personal identification numbers (PINs) or other sensitive information. If you have not requested information, do not open these emails. Never give your account or password information. Do not click on links in suspicious emails. Doing so could allow spyware on your phone or computer, which is another way for criminals to steal information.

For more information:

- Read the FTC article "How to Recognize and Avoid Phishing Scams" at www.consumer .ftc.gov/articles/how-recognize-and-avoid -phishing-scams.
- Check with the U.S. Securities and Exchange Commission at www.sec.gov or (800) 732-0330.

To file a complaint:

- Go to www.IC3.gov, the Internet Crime Complaint Center, and your state attorney general's office.

Identity Theft

Never give personal information (credit card number, driver's license number, Social Security number, birth date, mother's maiden name, etc.) unless you know who you are dealing with.

It's hard to know if you've been a victim of identity theft. Many times, your first knowledge of the theft is when charges appear on your credit card or you receive notification from a collection agency.

If you have been a victim of identity theft, contact the Federal Trade Commission Identity Theft Hotline at 1-877-IDTHEFT, or visit www .identitytheft.gov.

File a police report to submit to creditors and others that may require proof of the crime. Immediately call your financial institutions.

If you believe someone is using your Social Security number, call the Social Security Administration Fraud Hotline at 1-800-269-0271.

The following are steps you can take to prevent identity theft.

Be careful what you carry.

- Never leave your purse or wallet in your car.
- Only carry credit cards that you need, and carry no more than two at one time.
- Never carry your Social Security card or birth certificate.
- Carry your Medicare card only when visiting your doctor.
- Do not keep ATM PINs or passwords in your wallet.
- Carry your passport only when traveling.

Credit Cards

- Write *Ask for ID* instead of your signature on the back of your credit card.
- Ask your credit card issuer to add an instant transaction alert service on your account.

Records/Documentation

- At home, keep a list of all your credit and bank accounts. Include account numbers, expiration dates and telephone numbers of the customer service departments.
- Keep tax records, canceled checks and bills in a secure place, or shred them before throwing them away.
- Give your Social Security number only when necessary. Use other types of identification.

Mail

- Place outgoing mail containing personal information in a secure mailbox. Make sure your incoming mail is placed in a secure mailbox.
- Do not write account numbers on the outside of envelopes.

Checks

- If you write a check to pay your credit card bill, then do not put your full credit card number on your check; just put the last four digits.

PROTECTING YOURSELF FROM FRAUD

For elderly financial abuse, see Chapter 15.

- *Money Smart for Older Adults Resource Guide* provides information on common scams and frauds as well as steps you can take to avoid being targeted or victimized— www.files.consumerfinance.gov/f /documents/201703_cfpb_money-smart -for-older-adults-resource-guide.pdf

- Cybersecurity for mobile devices like smartphones and tablets— www.dhs.gov/stopthinkconnect

- Internet safety— www.fbi.gov/scams-and-safety

- Investment Fraud
  - www.sec.gov/spotlight/cybersecurity
  - www.serveourseniors.org

- Charity scams—www.ftc.gov/charity

- Medicare fraud—www.smpresource.org

- Romance fraud—www.consumer.ftc.gov /articles/what-you-need-know-about -romance-scams

- Do not have your Social Security or driver's license number printed on your checks.

Websites/Computers
- Make your passwords complicated, and regularly change them.
- Frequently update the virus and firewall protection on your computer.
- When you place orders on the internet, make sure you are using secure sites.
- Don't give personal information on social networks.
- Don't answer security questions honestly, such as birthplace, etc.

- Never assume that public Wi-Fi is secure. Do not pay bills or enter your username or passwords in public.
- Home aides and retirement home staff have access to records. Keep papers locked up.
- In an obituary, do not give a person's birth date and month, only the year, and do not include maiden names. Mail the death certificate to all three credit bureaus. Have them mark the record as deceased. Notify your state department of motor vehicles (DMV), and cancel the deceased's credit card(s) ASAP.

For more information, contact:
- **www.privacyrights.org**
- **www.fraud.org**
- **http://taxpayeradvocate.irs.gov/get-help /identity-theft.**

Rebates and Coupons

Rebates and coupons can save money, but they may not be for you. Some rebates and coupons are offered to introduce a new product, while others aim to sell a product that is overstocked. Decide if you really need the item; then, comparison shop. If you do buy, you'll then have the problem of applying for the rebate. For most rebates, the bar code from the product's package must be mailed in with a proof of purchase within a certain time. Many people simply do not follow through.

Tax Returns

If you use a commercial tax firm to file your income tax, don't agree to or sign a refund anticipation loan.

Some preparers call them rapid refunds. It sounds great, but you are losing money by paying a very high interest rate plus fees. The firms granting the loans make millions. Many taxpayers are unaware that their rapid refund is a loan. You do better financially to wait three to four weeks for IRS to mail or deposit your refund.

Take tax time as an opportunity to save. If you're receiving a refund, use your tax form to tell IRS to put the part you need right away into your checking account and automatically deposit the rest into your savings account. **Contact the IRS Taxpayer Advocate Service at www.taxpayeradvocate.irs .gov for help with tax problems.**

Leasing vs. Buying

Before you buy or lease a car, review your budget to determine how much you can afford. Has buying a car been part of your short-term savings goals?

When you lease a car, you spend less on a monthly basis than you would buying a car. But at the end of the lease, you don't own a car, and it may be hard to save enough to buy one. **To learn about financing options and to figure out if leasing fits your situation, read *Financing or Leasing a Car* at www.consumer.ftc.gov/articles/0056 -financing-or-leasing-car.**

Financing a Vehicle

Will you buy and, if so, how? You have two choices: pay in full or finance over time. In direct lending, you get a loan from a bank or credit union. In dealership financing, be aware that a car dealer may charge a markup for arranging your financing. You'll be repaying this through your monthly payments. Before buying:

- Check the current rates offered at a bank, at a credit union or on the internet. Compare those with the rate the dealer offers.
- Focus on the purchase price, not just the monthly payments.
- If you're financing with a dealership, bargain for a lower rate; the dealer sets it, and it can be changed.
- Never sign a blank loan document or a blank check.

Used Car Purchases

Typically, a car has depreciated to half of its original value after two years even though it may still have three-quarters of its life left. Verify the value of a car using Kelley Blue Book or Edmunds. **Read *Buying a Used Car* at www.consumer.ftc.gov /articles/0055-buying-used-car.**

Health Insurance Scams

Do not give your Medicare or health insurance information to someone who calls you unless you know them. If someone calls, emails or texts and says they're from the government, it's a scam. For example, scam operators call seniors asking for Medicare information in order to send a genetic testing kit in the mail. Medicare does not call beneficiaries. Medicare only covers one genetic test—Cologuard, which is a colorectal cancer screening test available only by prescription.

Some scam operators sell skimpy policies or medical discount plans where consumers pay a fee to get out-of-pocket discounted medical services. To avoid being scammed, get the salesperson's name, telephone number, address and business license. Call your state insurance department to ask if the company or agent is licensed to do business in the state and if any action has been taken against them.

No insurance representative should pressure you into making a decision on the spot. Never provide bank account or credit card information to get locked-in premiums. Read the insurance policy.

Health Care Hazards

Americans are vulnerable to health swindles because we are health-conscious and often assume that a remedy must be available for our ailments. People spend billions of dollars a year on fraudulent health products marketed as drugs or dietary supplements or medical devices.

The Food and Drug Administration (FDA) describes *health fraud* as "articles of unproven effectiveness that are promoted to improve health, well-being or appearance." Scammers promote their products through newspapers, magazines, direct mail and TV infomercials. You can find health fraud scams in stores and on countless websites, in popup ads and spam, and on social media sites like Facebook and Twitter.

The FDA suggests watching out for these red flags for fraudulent products and scam operators.

- Sounds too good to be true
- Relies on a "special" or "all-natural" formula or "secret" device
- Claims that methods are superior to those used by medical doctors or are an alternative to drugs or surgery
- Relies heavily on testimonials from patients or doctors played by actors
- Implies a quick fix or easy weight loss
- Claims to cure a wide range of unrelated diseases, particularly serious diseases such as cancer, diabetes and Alzheimer's. If a real cure for a serious disease were discovered, it would be widely reported through the media and prescribed by doctors.
- Promises money-back guarantees

Even with these tips, fraudulent health products are not always easy to spot. If you're tempted to buy an unproven product, check with your doctor first. Leave your diagnosis to your doctor, and only take medicines your doctor prescribes to you.

For more information from the FDA, go to www.fda.gov/healthfraud.

To search for FDA-approved prescription drugs, over-the-counter drugs (brand name and generic) and therapeutic biological products, go to www.fda.gov/drugs/drug-approvals-and -databases/about-drugsfda.

Tips to find reliable information online can be found at www.nia.nih.gov/health/online -health-information-it-reliable.

Stretching Health Care Dollars

You should not skimp on your health care, but there are steps you can take to reduce health care costs. Consider the following.

For routine care:
- Call or email to consult about minor health problems.

- Know which public health services are available for screening and detection of diseases.
- Find out about free clinics operated by service-oriented agencies.

For hospital care:
- Avoid confinement in the hospital for diagnostic tests and treatment that could be given as outpatient services.
- Do not insist on a private hospital room.
- Investigate the possibility of having the services of a visiting nurse before going to the hospital. Room and board are cheaper at home than at the hospital if you can receive the services you need in your home.
- Research group purchasing plans available to unions, consumer cooperatives and senior citizens.

For medicines:
The CDC reports that among adults age 65 and over who were prescribed medication, 5% did not take their medication as prescribed because they were trying to save money. Alternative ways to consider saving money include the following:

- Ask your doctor to write a generic prescription. A generic medicine works the same way as a brand-name version and can be much cheaper.
- Ask your doctor for a lower cost medicine.
- If you are not getting results, review the medication with your doctor to evaluate whether it is still needed or if there are any drug interactions that should be taken into account.
- Shop around. Prices can vary from pharmacy to pharmacy for the same medicines.
- Ask for a senior discount.
- Check internet and mail-order pharmacies for lower prices.
- If you take a drug regularly, check with your insurance plan to see if you can get a 90-day supply of your medication or if they offer a mail-order discount option.
- Check the pharmacy industry site at www .medicineassistancetool.org for possible patient assistance programs.

Hiring a Home Improvement Professional

Do your research.

- Check with friends, neighbors or co-workers for recommendations.

- Look at websites that post ratings and reviews like www.angieslist.com, www.homeadvisor.com or www.porch.com.

- Look for an established company that has been around for a long time.

- Make sure a contractor meets insurance, licensing and registration requirements.

Look for signs of a home improvement scam.

You may not want to do business with someone who:

- Knocks on your door for business or offers you discounts for finding other customers

- Just happens to have materials left over from a previous job

- Pressures you for an immediate decision

- Only accepts cash, asks you to pay everything up-front or suggests you borrow money from a lender the contractor knows

- Asks you to get the required building permits

- Tells you your job will be a "demonstration"

- Offers a lifetime warranty or long-term guarantee.

Understand your payment options.

- Don't pay cash.

- Try to limit your down payment. State laws vary.

- Try to make payments contingent upon completion of defined amounts of work. This way, if the work isn't going according to schedule, your payments also are delayed.

Before you sign off and make the final payment, check that:

- All work meets the standards spelled out in the contract

- You have written warranties for materials and workmanship

- You have proof that all subcontractors and suppliers have been paid

- The jobsite has been cleaned up

- You have inspected and approved the completed work.

Job and Business Opportunity Scams

Promises of a big income by working from home, especially when the "opportunity" involves an up-front fee or giving your credit card information, should make you very suspicious.

Beware these types of jobs and businesses:

- Reselling designer clothing, purses or perfumes
- Envelope stuffing
- Medical billing
- Mystery shopping
- Rebate processing
- Assembly or craft work
- Internet searching.

If you're thinking about following up on a work-at-home offer, do your research. It's a good idea to find out about other people's experiences. Try entering the company or promoter's name with the words "complaint," "reviews" or "scam" into a search engine.

Contact your local consumer protection agency, your state attorney general or the Better Business Bureau—not only where the company is located but also where you live—to see if they've received complaints. Ask the business opportunity promoter questions about the work, how you will be paid and the basis for claims about likely earnings.

How to File a Complaint

Know how and where to file a complaint when your consumer rights have been violated. It is worth the bother. When you report unsatisfactory goods or services, assemble all the information about dates, payments, contracts, receipts, etc., so that there is little room for confusion. This will demonstrate that you are serious about carrying through with your complaint.

If you cannot get satisfaction from a salesperson, find the highest authority to whom you can appeal in the store or on the phone. Keep calm. Maintaining your composure will show confidence, which can be helpful in these situations.

You might consider writing a letter to the president of a company. State the facts clearly, and keep a copy of everything for your records.

For complaints that cannot be settled using these measures, contact your state attorney general's office.

To report fraud, scams or unfair business practices, go to www.ftccomplaintassistant.gov or call (877) 382-4357.

To file a complaint about a financial product or service with the Consumer Financial Protection Bureau, go to www.consumerfinance .gov/complaint.

RESOURCES

Learn how to be a safe consumer when it comes to insurance, scams and unwanted mail at www.usa.gov/consumer.

Find your state's consumer protection office at www.usa.gov/state-consumer.

The *Consumer Action Handbook* has information on shopping for goods and services, knowing your consumer rights and learning how to file a complaint. It provides a consumer assistance directory, with contact information for government agencies and national corporations. Visit www.usa.gov/handbook.

To learn more about money, renting, mortgages, health and fitness, jobs, privacy and online security, visit www.consumer.ftc.gov.

Learn about consumer protection basics such as managing your money, using credit and loans, and protecting your identity and money at www.consumer.gov.

For updates and information on staying safe and healthy, visit www.fda.gov/consumers.

Living Longer and Better

"Often when you think you're at the end of something, you're at the beginning of something else."

—Fred Rogers

You've Got Your Health

Much of life is improved by having good health. Many people think that money is the most important part of retirement, but it is actually your health. If you are not healthy or able to enjoy activities, the amount of money you have becomes less important.

According to a UnitedHealthcare survey, older adults say health is the biggest factor to achieving their goals in retirement. The top retirement goals were seeking new experiences, being healthier and being social.

An added benefit of good health is that your health costs are reduced, you are more productive, and you can choose to work longer or have an active retirement.

The components of a healthy lifestyle include nutrition, activity, sleep, stress resilience and mental health care.

Mental and Physical Health

Mental health and physical health are closely connected. Mental health plays a major role in people's ability to maintain good physical health. In turn, illness and chronic physical health conditions can impact mental health. People with a healthy sense of self and social supports will not be completely protected from poor health, of course, but those who cope successfully with life's problems, not only during aging but throughout all of life, usually have more positive outcomes. Just as you have probably faced crises or problematic situations during your life, you will face them in retirement and cope with them as effectively as you did earlier.

Aging and Exercise

What happens to our bodies as we grow older?

Dr. Herbert A. de Vries, former director of the exercise laboratory of the Andrus Gerontology Center of the University of Southern California, outlined what happens to aging bodies.

- The heart's ability to pump blood declines by about 8% each decade in adulthood.
- Blood pressure increases as fatty deposits clog arteries. By middle age, the openings of the coronary arteries are likely to be about 29% smaller than when you were in your mid-20s.

Profile of Longevity

People most likely to succeed at living a long time:

- Understand themselves physically, mentally and socially
- Eat healthy
- Have strong family bonds
- Have good medical care and regular medical, dental and eye checkups
- Maintain positive attitudes and a sense of humor
- Show stress resilience and adapt to change
- Have a habit of daily exercise
- Enjoy rewarding personal relationships
- Keep a good environment, physically and mentally
- Set up good sleep habits
- Demonstrate a commitment to something other than themselves
- Have a willingness to try new things—e.g., a class, a musical instrument or a language
- Participate in community activities
- Are fortunate enough to have good genes.

People with the following traits tend to adjust to transitions and cope with change better than those who lack them.

- Enduring and honest affection for others
- Independence
- Satisfying outlets for time and energy
- Enjoyment of life
- Sense of usefulness
- Avoidance of self-pity.

A 2019 study found that people who tend to be optimistic are likelier than others to live to be 85 years old or more. Researchers from Boston University School of Medicine and the Harvard T. H. Chan School of Public Health say that this finding was independent of other factors thought to influence longevity. Optimistic people still have stress, but they tend to be more resilient. The good news is that optimism can be taught by learning to catch yourself in a pessimistic outlook and consciously shifting it.

For more information on living a long life, visit the Stanford Center on Longevity website at www.longevity.stanford.edu.

- Lung capacity decreases and the chest wall stiffens as you grow older. This cuts the amount of oxygen available to body tissues for work and other physical activities.
- Skeletal muscles, such as those in arms and legs, gradually lose strength. Tests show that 3% to 5% of muscle tissue is lost every decade. Loss of muscular strength and tissue means ebbing endurance.
- The proportion of your body that is fat increases. To keep the same proportion of fat to lean body mass (not the way you look outside, but internally), you have to weigh less and less as you grow older.

But don't let these facts about aging worry you too much! Keeping active can help you stay young in spite of your calendar years and can also help you feel better.

Researchers at the University of Birmingham and King's College London found that consistently exercising over the course of a lifetime slows the aging process, particularly for immunity and muscle mass. But even if you've been less active, there's a benefit to starting regular exercise later in life. Cardiologists at the University of Texas Southwestern Medical Center found that exercise can reverse damage to sedentary, aging hearts and help reduce the risk of future heart failure. These results were achieved with regular exercise (at least four times a week) beginning before age 65.

Exercise Is Good for You

Exercise and physical activity are good for you, no matter how old you are. Being active is one of the most important things you can do to maintain and improve health. To get the most out of exercise and physical activity, they need to be a regular part of your life.

Staying active can help you:
- Keep and improve your strength so that you can stay independent
- Have more energy to do the things you want to do
- Improve your balance and prevent falls
- Prevent or delay some diseases like heart disease, stroke, type 2 diabetes, osteoporosis and certain types of cancer
- Perk up your mood and reduce feelings of depression
- Sleep better at night
- Reduce levels of stress and anxiety
- Reach or maintain a healthy weight.

Four Ways to Be Active

To get all of the benefits of physical activity, try all four types of exercise:

- Endurance, or aerobic, activities increase your breathing and heart rate. They keep your heart, lungs and circulatory system healthy. Building your endurance makes it easier to carry out everyday activities. Endurance exercises include brisk walking, dancing and yard work (mowing, raking, digging).
- Strength exercises make your muscles stronger. They may help you perform everyday activities such as climbing stairs and carrying groceries. Strength exercises can include using your own body weight, resistance bands or hand weights.
- Balance exercises can help to prevent falls. Many lower body strength exercises will also improve your balance. Balance exercises include standing on one foot or the other and practicing Tai Chi.
- Flexibility exercises stretch your muscles and can help your body stay limber. Being flexible gives you more freedom of movement for other exercises as well as for your everyday activities, including driving and getting dressed. Flexibility exercises include stretching and yoga.

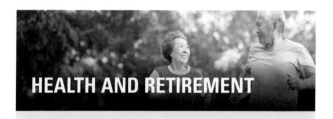

HEALTH AND RETIREMENT

Nearly 40% of the people who retired earlier than they planned did so because of health reasons, according to a report by the Center for Retirement Research at Boston College. Don't assume you can work into your 70s. Now is the time to take steps to get or stay healthy. The National Institutes of Health cites that losing weight can improve your blood pressure, cholesterol and blood sugar levels. It is important to eat healthy meals, maintain a healthy weight, get moving, take prescribed medications and find ways to relieve stress.

BENEFITS OF WALKING

Walking provides excellent exercise for the heart, muscles and lungs, and it gives you a chance to relax, enjoy your surroundings and give you a much-needed breath of fresh air.

Build up your walking distance slowly. Keep your pace fast but comfortable. Increase the distance you walk up to 45 minutes. Wear a good pair of sneakers that fit well. Check with your doctor about any concerns.

Local fitness centers or hospitals might be able to help you find a physical activity program that works for you. You also can check with nearby senior centers, religious or community centers, parks, recreation associations or even area shopping malls for exercise, wellness or walking programs.

Get Moving Wisely

See your doctor before you start an exercise or activity program. Your doctor may have advice to share with you. People with chronic health conditions typically can exercise as long as they're monitored by a doctor.

Don't overdo exercise, particularly at the beginning. It takes more than a day for people to get out of shape, and it may take a while before you build up endurance, strength, balance and flexibility. Exercise programs can be created for anyone—the middle-aged, the healthy, the infirm and those with special health needs. Sit-down exercises for people who are sedentary are particularly important, as are exercises for the bedridden.

Here are some things you can do to make sure you are exercising safely:

- Start slowly, especially if you haven't been active for a long time. Little by little, build up your activities and how hard you work at them.
- Don't hold your breath during strength exercises. That could cause changes in your blood pressure. It may seem strange at first, but you should breathe out as you lift something and breathe in as you relax.
- Use safety equipment. For example, wear a helmet for bike riding and the right shoes for walking.
- Unless your doctor has asked you to limit fluids, be sure to drink plenty of fluids when you are doing activities, even if you don't feel thirsty.
- Always bend forward from the hips, not the waist. Keep your back straight.
- Warm up your muscles before you stretch. Try walking and light arm pumping first.
- Exercise should not hurt or make you feel really tired. You might feel some soreness, a little discomfort or a bit weary, but you should not feel pain. In fact, in many ways, being active will probably make you feel better.

Fitting Activity Into Your Day

Don't let a busy day stop you from exercising! You are more likely to exercise if it's a convenient part of your day. Here are some ideas:

- Schedule 30 minutes of exercise every day on your calendar.
- Walk the entire mall or every aisle of the grocery store when you go shopping.
- Try being active first thing in the morning before you get too busy.
- Take the stairs instead of escalators or elevators.
- Find an "exercise buddy" to help hold yourself accountable and add a social element to your fitness.
- Take a walk during lunch with co-workers or friends.
- Use family gatherings as a time to play team sports or do outdoor activities.

For exercise ideas, videos and motivational tips, visit www.go4life.nia.nih.gov.

Healthy Eating

Together, healthy eating and regular physical activity can help people:

- Achieve and maintain a healthy weight
- Reduce the risk of obesity. Obesity is a major risk factor for several diseases.
- Reduce the risk of heart disease and stroke
- Reduce the risk of certain forms of cancer
- Strengthen muscles, bones and joints
- Improve mood and energy level.

About half of all American adults have one or more preventable chronic diseases, many of which are related to physical inactivity and poor quality in terms of eating patterns. This shows that many people need to make some changes in their food and beverage choices to achieve a healthy eating pattern. Talk to your doctor. Making a plan to eat better can keep you healthy and active for longer.

Choose lean meats, fruits, vegetables and foods with fiber such as whole grains and legumes. Choose "good" or unsaturated fats. These turn down inflammation, which can cause damage to your body.

Limit sugar and foods high in saturated fat. Sweet foods and drinks can cause blood sugar spikes that can make you hungry sooner and lead to the development of many types of diseases.

Find more information on the following topics:

- **Smart food choices—www.nia.nih.gov /health/smart-food-choices-healthy-aging**
- **Healthy eating and shopping tips— www.nia.nih.gov/health/healthy-eating**

Eating Concerns for Older Adults

Eating habits change as our bodies get older. Older adults may have special nutrition plans to treat a chronic condition like diabetes, and this can be even more difficult for those on a fixed income. And people from all walks of life face challenges to healthy eating and drinking enough water. Challenges and solutions include:

TAKE BREAKS FROM SITTING

As technology has advanced in recent decades, so has sitting. Too many hours of sitting raises risks for obesity, diabetes, cardiovascular disease, deep-vein thrombosis and metabolic syndrome. Sitting less is important to a healthy lifestyle. A study from the American Cancer Society finds a link between long periods (six or more hours a day) of leisure time sitting and a higher risk of death from all causes. Risks of death among those who reported the most leisure time sitting were higher for cancer, coronary heart disease, stroke, diabetes, kidney disease, suicide, lung disease, liver disease, peptic ulcer and other digestive diseases, Parkinson's disease, Alzheimer's disease, nervous disorders and musculoskeletal disorders.

According to Harvard HEALTHbeat, researchers aren't sure why prolonged sitting has such harmful health consequences. But one possible explanation is that it relaxes your largest muscles. Relaxed muscles take up very little glucose from the blood, raising your risk of type 2 diabetes. Sitting can also increase pain, tighten the hip flexor and hamstring muscles and stiffen joints. Following are ways to avoid sitting too long.

- Set a timer to remind yourself to get up and move around every so often.
- Sit on a stability ball, which makes you use your muscles to stay upright.
- At home, get up and do something instead of skipping through TV commercial breaks.
- At work, use the farthest bathroom from your desk.

- Not feeling hungry: Reduced appetite could be part of the aging process where you need fewer calories because of a slowing metabolism and less physical activity, but weight loss is not a normal part of aging. Lack of appetite could be due to medication, depression or other challenges listed in the following bullet points. Sticking to a regular eating schedule can help your brain to signal hunger. Instead of trying to eat more food, add healthy, nutrient-dense foods like avocados, olive oil, and nut or seed butters to your meals.

- Losing a sense of thirst: Drink water throughout the day. Drink a full glass any time you take medication.
- Chewing: Problems with teeth, gums and dentures can make it hard to chew fruits, vegetables or meats. Eating softer foods can help. Try cooked or canned foods like unsweetened fruit, beans, tuna, frozen vegetables that steam in the microwave and soups.
- Foods seem to lose flavor: Maybe your sense of smell, sense of taste or both have changed. Medicines may also change how foods taste or cause digestive side effects that make you avoid foods you used to enjoy. Add flavor to your meals with herbs, spices, lemon juice and vinegar.
- Being tired of cooking or eating alone: Schedule potlucks with friends and family. If everyone brings one part of the meal, cooking is a lot easier, and there might be leftovers to share. Or try cooking with a friend to make a meal you can enjoy together. Also look into having some meals at a nearby senior center or other place in the community. Meals can be more enjoyable when you eat with others.
- Losing mobility and strength: If you're having difficulty shopping or lifting heavy groceries, find out if grocery delivery is an option. Ask a neighbor to shop for you. People with arthritis may be unable to lift heavy pots or pans, cut with a knife and/or unwrap packaged food. Microwaving frozen meals may be an option.

Resources on nutrition include:
- **Problem-solving suggestions for roadblocks to healthy eating—www.nia.nih.gov/health/overcoming-roadblocks-healthy-eating**

- **Healthy, Delicious Food at Every Age—www.harvardpilgrim.org/public/docs/healthy-delicious-food**
- **Tips for getting enough fluids—www.nia.nih.gov/health/getting-enough-fluids**

A Good Night's Sleep

What time you get to bed isn't as important as how long you stay there. Recognize that sleep needs differ. You may be among those who need more or less than the norm of 7½ hours.

Getting enough sleep can help you:
- Become sick less often
- Maintain a healthy weight
- Lower your risk for serious health problems
- Reduce stress and improve your mood
- Think more clearly
- Get along better with people
- Make good decisions and avoid injuries; for example, sleepy drivers cause thousands of car accidents every year.

On the other hand, too much sleep is associated with many health conditions, including type 2 diabetes, heart disease and depression.

Suggestions for healthy sleep habits include:
- Avoid naps, especially in the afternoon.
- Go to bed and get up about the same time every day, weekends included.
- If you go to bed and don't feel sleepy, try to lull yourself to sleep with a calming activity such as reading or turning on quiet, soothing music.
- Avoid or limit coffee, tea or other caffeine products, alcohol and nicotine in the afternoon or evening. Alcohol may help you go to sleep, but it can cause you to wake up throughout the night.
- Do not exercise rigorously within five to six hours of bedtime.
- In the evening, avoid eating heavy or spicy meals or drinking too many liquids.
- Do not watch TV or any electronic screen in bed. For some people, laptop and phone

screens can make it hard to fall asleep because the particular type of light emanating from the screens of these devices activates the brain.

■ Sleep in a quiet and dark room. Use a sound machine or a fan to block noise, and install darkening blinds.

■ Don't try to force sleep. The more you struggle to sleep or worry about wakefulness, the harder it will be to get to sleep. It can be better to stay awake a while longer and just relax.

Insomnia

Most of us have experienced brief periods of difficulty falling asleep or staying asleep.

But frequent, long-lasting problems with sleep indicate a need to see your doctor. If nothing else, it is better to be assured that you have nothing to worry about than to find out later that you have a problem that requires professional treatment. Doctors consider insomnia chronic if symptoms like difficulty falling or staying asleep, fatigue, irritability and/or difficulty concentrating occur at least three nights per week for three months or longer.

Experts have found that many chronic insomniacs keep their problems bottled up inside instead of venting anger, frustrations and disappointments. The build-up of tension, stress and anxiety can be carried into the night and are likely to cause racing thoughts, activate physical systems and make it difficult to get to sleep.

Chronic insomnia often can be traced to illnesses. See your doctor about treatment options before taking any kind of sleep aid medication.

For more information, go to:
■ **www.sleepfoundation.org**
■ **www.sleepeducation.org.**

Stop Smoking

Smoking is not as prevalent as it once was. Only about 14% of adults are current cigarette

MEDITATION FOR SLEEP

Meditation, a deep relaxation technique, has been shown to increase sleep time, improve sleep quality and make it easier to fall asleep. Not only can meditation improve your sleep quality, but it may also help with health conditions that worsen with stress. Lie down, close your eyes, and breathe slowly and deeply, directing your attention to follow your breath as you inhale and exhale. If your mind starts to wander, simply bring your attention back to your breath, without judgment.

smokers. If you still smoke, now's the time to join the millions of ex-smokers. Smoking is an expensive habit, both in terms of your health and your wealth. It's responsible for more cancer-related deaths than any other single agent, and it's a contributing factor in emphysema, bronchitis and heart attacks.

If you are a smoker and want to quit, accentuate the positive and focus on the benefits of quitting.

When you quit smoking, your body starts to repair itself almost immediately. You enter lower risk health groups. You lose your smoker's hacking cough and related headaches and stomachaches. You recover your sense of taste and smell.

If you want to quit smoking, the American Cancer Society has information to help you. Go to www.cancer.org/healthy.

AARP reports many older smokers are switching to vaping, usually in the form of e-cigarettes, as a way to reduce tobacco use. Vaping can cause mouth or throat irritation, nausea and coughing, and the long-term effects are not yet known.

The FDA has not approved e-cigarettes as a way to quit smoking.

Warning of a Stroke

Stroke is the third leading cause of death and the No. 1 cause of adult disability in the United States. Knowing the warning signs and getting quick treatment are critical to treating a stroke.

Be aware of the following signs.

- Unexplained weakness, tingling or numbness in the face, arm or leg, usually on one side of the body
- Difficulty speaking or understanding words
- Changes in vision such as blurred or decreased vision
- Severe headache, sometimes with nausea or vomiting
- Dizziness or difficulty with walking or coordination

If you or others experience any of these symptoms, call 911 immediately.

Living With Stress

Stress is the body's physical and chemical reaction to anything that frightens, excites, confuses or endangers us. Here's some of what happens in a stress response. The brain tells the muscles to tighten and the blood vessels to constrict. The brain also tells the adrenal glands to release stress hormones to get more oxygen to your muscles and give your cells more energy. To accommodate these needs, your heart beats faster and your blood pressure goes up.

This reaction isn't harmful to your body if it occurs once in a while. However, prolonged and excessive stress has a connection to a variety of health conditions. Stress can weaken the immune system and increase blood pressure and the risk of heart disease. Stress also can lead to anxiety, depression, trouble with sleeping and digestive problems.

People approaching retirement and retirees are more vulnerable to stress. Research shows that the aging body has a diminishing ability to respond to stress as we grow older. Stress hits the body harder, and recovery takes longer. Finding ways to reduce stress can help you stay healthy.

HEARING LOSS

Hearing loss is one of the most common conditions affecting older adults, and the timing could occur earlier than expected. Hearing loss often goes untreated. If hearing loss is gradual, you might not notice the problem. Some people don't want to face the problem or its treatment because of stigma. Even among people who are aware of their hearing loss, only about 20% wear hearing aids. Cost and technical difficulties are barriers too, since Medicare doesn't pay for hearing aids. Getting the settings right also can be a frustrating process.

Untreated hearing loss is linked to loneliness, which raises the risk of depression and dementia. Research shows that loneliness also can lead to high blood pressure, elevated stress hormones and weakened immune systems.

Tell your friends and family about your hearing loss. The more people you tell, the more people there will be to help you cope and practice strategies like lip reading. It will take time for friends and family to get used to speaking louder and more clearly. It's hard to be open and patient, but hearing better is worth the effort to stay socially connected.

For more about age-related hearing loss, go to www.nidcd.nih.gov/health/age -related-hearing-loss.

For hearing aid financial assistance options, go to www.hearingloss.org/hearing-help /financial-assistance.

While stress is a normal part of life, lots of people need help dealing with stress. Don't feel ashamed, embarrassed or guilty about getting help—It's not an admission of personal inadequacy but a mark of intelligence to seek professional advice.

How You Think About Stress

The previous section noted some harmful health effects of the stress response on the body. Health psychologist Kelli McGonigal presented a TED Talk in 2013 called "How to Make Stress Your Friend," in which she suggested that the harmful effects of stress are not inevitable. She explained how the new science of stress reveals that if you change your mind about stress, you can change your body's response to stress.

Changing your mind looks like this: When you feel the stress response in your body, don't think stress is the enemy. Instead, think, this is my body helping me rise to this challenge, giving me the extra strength needed to achieve more—to endure more, work harder and work more creatively.

Participants in a study conducted at Harvard University were taught to rethink their stress response as helpful before they went through a social stress test. For example, a pounding heart is preparing you for action. Breathing faster is no problem because it's getting more oxygen to your brain. The physical stress response changed for participants who viewed the stress response as helpful for their performance in the social stress test. Their heart was still pounding, but their blood vessels stayed relaxed instead of constricting. The blood vessels looked a lot like what happens in moments of joy and courage. McGonigal said, "Over a lifetime of stressful experiences, this one biological change could be the difference between a stress-induced heart attack at age 50 and living well into your 90s."

McGonigal's second insight about stress response is that it makes people social because it releases the hormone oxytocin, sometimes known as the "cuddle hormone," in response to social bonding. When oxytocin is released in the stress response, it motivates you to seek support and tell someone how you feel. When you notice someone else in your life is struggling, your stress response triggers you to support him or her. "When life is difficult, your stress response wants you to be surrounded by people who care about you," she said. In addition,

oxytocin helps regenerate heart cells that may have been damaged by stress.

McGonigal concludes, "How you think and how you act can transform your experience of stress. When you choose to view your stress response as helpful, you create the biology of courage. And when you choose to connect with others under stress, you can create resilience."

Signs of Stress

Stress is different for everyone. Recognizing the signs of stress is the first step toward coping with it effectively. Unfortunately, too many of us do not recognize the signs of stress or pay too little attention to them. Review the signs and test your stress level on page 84.

Causes of Stress

Change is often a cause of stress.

The death or serious illness of a spouse is considered by psychologists to be the most serious cause of stress. Seek help for stress caused by the loss of a spouse or the death of a close relative or friend.

Other common causes of stress include:
- Retirement (because of the upheaval it causes in personal lives)
- Caregiving
- Financial problems
- Illness and accidents
- Marital troubles and divorce
- Sexual difficulties
- Work-related problems
- Changes in living conditions.

Even positive changes like getting a job promotion or having a baby or new grandchild can be stressful.

If you can isolate the cause of your stress, work out a solution. If there are a number of causes, work on them one at a time, starting with the most important first. It also can help to learn to accept that you cannot change problems that are beyond your control.

TEST YOUR STRESS LEVEL Score Yourself: Never = 0; Seldom = 1; Frequently = 2

How often do you feel:		How often do you experience:	
Strong anxiety	_____	General fatigue	_____
Irritable over little things	_____	Sleeplessness at night	_____
Frustrated	_____	Heart pounding	_____
Quick anger	_____	Headaches	_____
A desire to avoid people	_____	Breathing difficulties	_____
Difficulty in concentrating	_____	Digestive problems	_____
Easily disturbed or startled	_____	Frequent need to urinate	_____
Jittery, unable to sit still	_____	Tense head and neck muscles	_____
Unusually emotional	_____	Grinding of teeth	_____
Depressed	_____	Dry mouth or throat	_____
A loss of interest in everything	_____	Sudden perspiration	_____
Persistently nervous	_____	Emotional eating	_____

Add the point totals in the two columns: If together they are 10 or under, you are managing stress well; if 10 to 20, you have moderate stress; if higher, you could have major stress.

How to Ease Stress? Resilience

Resilience is the process of successfully bouncing back from stress—and it can be learned and developed in anyone. Here's how to get started.

Reframe Challenges as an Opportunity to Grow
There will always be unexpected bumps in the road, but reframing challenges can make a big difference in how you face a situation. Try to stay flexible to life's inevitable surprises. Resilient people are not paralyzed by challenges but instead see them as a chance to grow.

Improve Your Self-Talk
That little voice in your head? Make sure it's practicing self-compassion. A good way to tell if your self-talk needs a makeover is to consider whether you would say those same words to a friend in your situation. Try to stop negative self-talk when you hear it. Remember that everyone experiences struggles, and be optimistic about the future.

Establish Realistic Goals
In a crisis, it may be daunting to see how you will handle a problem. Try to view the situation in a matter-of-fact way and set reasonable goals. If you're getting overwhelmed, break the challenges down to small, manageable steps. You can do it!

Accept That Some Circumstances Are Outside of Your Control
Flexibility is an essential part of resilience, and it is sometimes necessary to adapt to a situation that you cannot control. Accept that reality, remain positive and focus your energy on situations that you can control.

Connect With Family, Friends, Co-Workers and Neighbors
Having a strong support network is a great way to get through life's challenges. Sharing your feelings with others allows you to release stress and brainstorm solutions, and a strong network can

provide both emotional and logistical support in a crisis. If your network isn't as large as you'd like, look for opportunities to help others. By extending support to others, you're more likely to receive support in return.

Know That Your Actions Are in Your Control

Don't forget that, ultimately, you are the one in the driver's seat of your life and the one in control of your future. Remember: You can't always choose what happens to you, but you can always choose how you respond.

Gratitude

Taking the time to feel gratitude may improve your emotional well-being by helping you cope with stress and increase positive emotions. The first step in any gratitude practice is to reflect on the good things that have happened in your life. These can be big or little things. It can be as simple as scoring a good parking space that day. Or, perhaps you feel grateful for a close friend's compassionate support.

Next, allow yourself a moment to enjoy that you had the positive experience, no matter what negatives may exist in your life. Developing a daily gratitude habit can help you learn to recognize good things in your life despite the bad things that might be happening.

Mindfulness

The practice of mindfulness is about being completely aware of what's happening in the present—of all that's going on inside and all that's happening around you. Mindfulness encourages you to pay attention to your thoughts and feelings as they are, without judgment or preconceived notions.

When you focus on your breathing, it's normal to realize how much your mind races and focuses on the past and future. You can just notice those thoughts and then return to the present moment. Your thoughts are bubbles waiting to be popped.

Studies suggest that mindfulness practices may help people manage stress, cope better with serious illnesses, and reduce anxiety and depression. Many people who practice mindfulness report an increased ability to relax and sleep, a greater enthusiasm for life and improved self-esteem.

This is likely because mindfulness tells the brain to do the opposite of the stress response. The relaxation response helps lower blood pressure, heart rate, breathing rate and stress hormones. Here are some ways to get started.

- Take some deep breaths. Breathe in through your nose to a count of four, hold for one second and then exhale through the mouth to a count of five. Repeat throughout the day for at least one minute at a time.
- Guided meditation. Look for a class in your area, or try an app like Insight Timer, Calm, Headspace or 10% Happier.
- Mindful walking. As you walk, notice your breath, your feet on the ground, and the sights and sounds around you. As thoughts and worries enter your mind, note them but then return to the present.
- Mindful eating. Be aware of taste, textures and flavors in each bite, and listen to your body when you are hungry and full.

BENEFITS OF LAUGHING

- Relaxes the whole body, relieving physical stress
- Boosts the immune system
- Releases endorphins, the body's natural feel-good chemicals, to reduce stress and pain
- Stops distressing emotions
- Increases blood flow and improves blood vessel function

Self-Compassion

Self-compassion involves showing kindness and understanding toward yourself when you are having a difficult time, fail or feel inadequate, rather than ignoring your pain or getting angry with yourself. Self-compassionate people recognize that being imperfect, failing and experiencing life's difficulties are an inevitable part of being human. We all will face frustrations and losses, make mistakes, and fall short of our ideals. Self-compassion means that you honor and accept your humanness. **For more information, go to www.self-compassion.org.**

Other Ways to Reduce Stress

What works best to reduce stress is different for everyone. Here are some more ideas:

- Making healthy lifestyle adjustments to your food choices, physical activity and sleep habits, as described in this chapter, will reduce stress.
- Slow down. Don't rush your life away. As a cardiologist put it, don't let yourself become a heart-attack-prone person—one who is hurried, aggressive, impatient and easily angered. A more relaxed person lives a far more pleasant and healthy life.
- Rid yourself of trivial obligations. Concentrate on what is most important to you.
- If you have a lot of things on your plate, create a to-do list and figure out what's most important—and then do that thing first.
- In retirement, recognize that boredom from inactivity is stressful.
  - Cultivate diversions such as exercise, concerts, museums and visits with friends.
  - The concentration needed for chess or some other game, a crossword puzzle or reading can help.
- Learn to enjoy your own company. It might be better to do nothing rather than rush to keep up with a full calendar.

Feeling Sad

Sadness is one of the most common and natural human emotions. Feeling sad is normal in response to loss and life's struggles. Provided you have times when you can enjoy things, however, this sadness is not a sign of depression. Often, the sad feelings resolve as you come to terms with the changes in your life. When sadness becomes overwhelming, lasts for long periods of time or causes symptoms of depression, people need medical help.

What Is Depression?

Depression is a common disease that is evidenced by excessive sadness, loss of interest in enjoyable things and low motivation. Depression is an illness, not a sign of weakness. Effective treatments are available.

What Are the Signs of Depression?

There are many symptoms of depression. Some of the most common are listed here. If you have several of these symptoms for more than two weeks, you may have depression. Recognizing the symptoms is key to helping yourself, a family member or a friend.

- Feeling miserable. Overwhelming sadness is present for much of the day and lasts for weeks.
- Loss of interest or pleasure in usual activities
- Irritability
- Trouble concentrating, remembering details and making decisions
- Recurring unpleasant thoughts, particularly about being guilty, worthless, helpless or hopeless
- Loss of appetite or overeating
- Loss of interest in sex
- Loss of energy, even when not physically active
- Loss of sleep despite feeling exhausted. Some people may sleep a lot more than usual.
- Slowed activity and speech
- Aches, pains, headaches or cramps that won't go away
- Digestive problems that don't get better, even with treatment
- Suicidal thoughts or attempts

Suicide

The National Suicide Prevention Lifeline offers free and confidential emotional support to people in suicidal crisis or emotional distress, as well as to friends and family members of people in distress.

■ www.suicidepreventionlifeline.org

■ 1-800-273-8255

Across the country, suicide rates have been on the rise, and that rise has struck senior citizens particularly hard. Men who are 65 and older face the highest risk of suicide, while adults 85 and older, regardless of gender, are the second most likely age group to die from suicide.

Seniors are at risk for suicide primarily because of loneliness. Another factor is isolation due to the death of a spouse, close family or friends. Physical limitations might end an older adult's ability to drive, read, engage in conversation, stay independent or find meaning.

Experts say there are certain "red flag" behaviors, including stockpiling medication, rushing to revise a will, increasingly using alcohol or drugs, altering sleep habits, sharing statements of hopelessness, withdrawing socially, saying goodbye or expressing the feeling of being a burden.

Health care for mental and physical conditions, social connections and skills for coping with transitions and adapting to change may help to protect against suicide risk in older adults.

For more information on suicide prevention, go to the American Foundation for Suicide Prevention at www.afsp.org.

Unfortunately, about half the people who have depression never get it diagnosed or treated. Half the people who have had one episode of depression will have a recurrence. If you or someone you know has had depression, act upon early warning signs because early treatment may decrease the severity of a depressive episode.

What Causes Depression?

No one knows exactly what causes depression. Depression seems to run in families. Stressful life events play a part. Stressful events can include financial difficulties, retirement, unemployment, childbirth, loneliness, or loss of someone or something important. Changes in the brain play a part. There are millions, even billions, of chemical reactions that make up the brain system that is responsible for your mood and how you perceive life experiences. Personality characteristics are a factor. Some people have a tendency to view themselves and the world negatively. Other possible causes of depression that should not be overlooked are medical conditions or side effects from medications. Talk to your doctor.

Depression Treatment

People with depression need help. There are many ways to deal with depression. Here are two of them.

Cognitive Behavioral Therapy (CBT)

This is a talk therapy in which negative patterns of thought about the self and the world are challenged, with the goal of altering unwanted behavior patterns and solving problems. It is the most widely used evidence-based practice aimed at improving mental health.

CBT involves learning skills to:

- Control negative thoughts
- Reduce the emotions of sadness and hopelessness
- Counteract behavior-related symptoms like poor concentration.

DEPRESSION IN OLDER ADULTS

Depression is a common problem among older adults, but it is not a normal part of aging.

Depression in older adults may be difficult to recognize because they may show different signs than younger people. Sadness may not be an older adult's main symptom. Tiredness, trouble sleeping and irritability are more common symptoms.

Confusion or attention problems caused by depression can sometimes look like Alzheimer's disease or other brain disorders.

Depression in older adults may have different causes compared with younger people. Older adults also may have more medical conditions, such as heart disease, stroke or cancer, which may cause depressive symptoms along with medication side effects that can contribute to depression.

For more information from the National Institute on Aging, go to www.nia.nih.gov /health/depression-and-older-adults.

Medication

Different antidepressant medications work in different ways. They take different lengths of time to start relieving symptoms. You may need to try more than one type of medication to find the one that works best for you. Keep in close contact with your doctor about side effects during the early stages of taking medication. Some things to remember when taking antidepressant medication include the following.

- Take the medication daily.
- Don't stop the medication, even if you feel better, without contacting the health professional who prescribed it.
- Side effects lessen as your body adjusts. If the side effects are too harsh, talk to your doctor.

Doctor's Visit

A correct diagnosis may depend on what you tell your doctor. Good communication with your doctor can improve health outcomes, life satisfaction and motivation to change unhealthy behaviors. Be open and honest with your doctor. Try the following to make the most of your doctor visits.

- Report health concerns.
- Freely exchange information, and ask questions. Prepare your questions before your visit.
- To prevent negative drug interactions, tell your doctor and pharmacist about all of the medications (prescription and over the counter) and dietary supplements you take.
- When you have a complaint or diagnosis, bring a spouse, family member or friend with you to the visit. Ask that person to take notes while you listen to the doctor.
- Ask the doctor when you should take your medicine and about possible side effects.
- Participate in treatment choices.
- Ask the doctor to explain medical jargon.
- Have the doctor summarize the visit.

For more information, go to www.nia.nih.gov /health/doctor-patient-communication/talking -with-your-doctor.

Checklist for
Health

Do you ...
Yes No

Eating

○ ○ Eat a balanced diet that includes lean meat, fish, fruits, vegetables and whole grains?

○ ○ Limit your intake of salt, sugar, fat and red meat?

○ ○ Limit caffeine and alcohol to two drinks per day?

○ ○ Make mealtime a pleasure?

○ ○ Wash your hands?

Physical activity

○ ○ Maintain a healthy weight?

○ ○ Exercise regularly?

○ ○ Know that exercise is the single best thing you can do for your brain in terms of mood, memory and learning?

○ ○ Take breaks from sitting?

○ ○ Sleep well?

Doctor visits

○ ○ Have regular medical and dental checkups? Come prepared with written concerns and questions?

○ ○ Ask about possible side effects of proposed treatments or medications?

○ ○ Keep a list of your medications and bring it to your doctor visits?

○ ○ Tell your doctor your family health history?

○ ○ Have your bone density screened?

○ ○ Have your vision and hearing checked every year?

Mental health

○ ○ Laugh frequently?

○ ○ Practice mindfulness?

○ ○ Cope with stress through resiliency?

○ ○ Get treatment for depression?

○ ○ Participate in community activities?

○ ○ Keep active through activities like reading and attending discussions and cultural events?

Health Insurance

"The first wealth is health."

—Ralph Waldo Emerson

Paying for Medical Expenses

Health insurance protects you from health and financial risks. No one plans to get sick or hurt, but most people need medical care at some point, and health insurance helps to cover these costs. Health insurance can help to finance the care you need to maintain good health.

The strategy behind health insurance is to spread health care costs across a large number of people. When any one person in a group health plan has a large medical bill, the cost of that person's treatment is funded by the premiums paid by everyone in that same risk pool.

Medicare

In conjunction with Social Security, Medicare plays a vital role in providing financial security to seniors. Medicare is a government-sponsored health insurance program available to Americans age 65 and older (and certain people on disability). The role of Medicare in society has evolved since it was signed into law in 1965. Originally conceived to simply provide reimbursement for medical expenses, Medicare today covers a huge population of Americans and is the biggest player in how medical care is provided.

Medicare plans are available in two types: Original Medicare and Medicare Advantage. Understanding the differences will help you make the right choice about how you are going to protect your health.

Original Medicare, which includes Parts A and B, is operated by the federal government. The government pays for your claims.

- Part A covers hospital, skilled nursing care, hospice and certain follow-up care after you leave the hospital. (**See page 92.**)
- Part B covers outpatient services and doctor visits. (**See page 92.**)
  - Prescription drug coverage is not included with Original Medicare.
  - Medigap plans supplement Parts A and B. (**See page 93.**)
- Part D covers drugs through private companies approved by Medicare. (**See page 97.**)

Part C is called Medicare Advantage and is an all-in-one alternative to Original Medicare. (**See page 98.**)

Note: Although full retirement age for Social Security benefits is increasing, Medicare is still available at age 65.

Medicare Part A (Hospital Insurance)

Hospital services include semiprivate rooms, meals, general nursing, drugs as part of inpatient treatment, and other hospital services and supplies. This includes the care provided in acute care hospitals, critical care hospitals, inpatient rehabilitation facilities, long-term care hospitals, inpatient care as part of a qualifying clinical research study and mental health care.

Part A is available premium-free to all qualified enrollees. Medicare Part A is available to anyone who is eligible for Social Security benefits and has (or their spouse has) made payroll tax contributions for ten or more years. You do not have to retire to get hospital insurance. It is available free at age 65, but you must enroll. Check with your Social Security office three months before you reach age 65.

People who have not worked long enough to qualify for Social Security can buy Medicare Part A insurance by paying a $437 monthly premium.

Medicare Part B (Medical Insurance)

Medicare Part B supplements Part A and covers doctor visits, outpatient hospital care, laboratory tests, preventive services and durable medical equipment. You pay a monthly premium for this coverage and an annual deductible of $198 before Medicare pays. Medicare pays for 80% of the approved amount for the cost of the service, and you pay the remaining 20% (coinsurance). Copayments may apply. There is no yearly limit for what you pay out of pocket.

Many screening tests are reimbursed, especially if your doctor recommends them, but you may be responsible for payment if a test isn't covered.

Under Original Medicare, doctors are restricted in how much they can charge Medicare patients. It should be noted that doctors are not required to see Medicare patients.

MEDICARE BENEFITS

With Medicare Part B, you are able to get a yearly wellness visit and many preventive services for no fee.

- For all Medicare benefits, go to www .medicare.gov/what-medicare-covers.

- Also see *Medicare & You* at www.medicare.gov/pubs/pdf/10050 -Medicare-and-You.pdf.

Key Enrollment Dates

Medicare Part B enrollment can be confusing because the key deadlines are customized to your birthday and depend on whether or not you are working at age 65. Missing the initial enrollment period is the biggest mistake people make when enrolling in Medicare. Here's how to avoid penalties.

Those who have opted for early retirement benefits under Social Security or Railroad Retirement are automatically enrolled in Medicare Part B when they reach age 65. Monthly premiums are deducted from Social Security checks.

- Medicare Part B has a seven-month initial enrollment period. This period begins three months before you turn 65. For example, if you turn 65 on April 11, the enrollment period begins January 1 and lasts until July 31. Sign up in the period three months before you turn 65 or three months after the month you turn 65 if you're not working, or else you will pay a penalty.

- If you are age 65 or older and you or your spouse are still working and receiving health coverage through an employer or union, you will need to sign up for Part B within eight months of leaving the job, or you will pay a penalty. If you or your spouse work for a small employer, the Part B enrollment rules are different. (**See page 102.**) Contact the administrator of your benefits to learn how your insurance works with Medicare.

■ Part D and Medicare Advantage plans require enrollment within 63 days of leaving the job to avoid penalties.

Late Enrollment Penalty

If you do not sign up for Part B and then decide you want it after your initial enrollment period ends (seven months if you are not working, or eight months after you stop working), you can sign up during a general enrollment period—January 1 through March 31 of each year. The penalty for enrolling during the general enrollment period is that your premium will be 10% higher for each 12-month period you could have been enrolled but were not. Also, your medical insurance protection won't start until the following July.

Tips for Making Medicare Decisions

Picking a Medicare plan is something that usually requires guidance and advice. It is complicated.

■ There is a wide range of premium levels and associated out-of-pocket costs among the plans.

■ Many insurance companies sell Medicare Advantage plans, Medigap plans and prescription drug plans. Each of these companies has multiple options of each plan.

■ A qualified Medicare insurance broker is likely in the best position to present all the options. Medicare brokers are paid by insurance companies.

Medicare Marketing

Companies aggressively market their plans.

■ Prior to turning 65, you may begin receiving many mailings about Medicare. A lot of them are ads. Mail will come from Social Security, insurance companies, agents, and organizations like AARP and those offering educational seminars. It can be overwhelming.

■ As you're reaching age 65 (or if you're over 65 and still working while covered by employer health insurance), pay attention to any mail reminding you of enrollment deadlines. (**See page 92.**)

Medicare Supplement (Medigap)

It is important to note that Medicare Part A and Medicare Part B (Original Medicare) benefits do not cover all health care costs. In many cases, these additional costs can be quite substantial. A Medigap policy is private health insurance that helps pay some of the health care costs that

Premium: Fee you pay to be covered by an insurance plan.

Deductible: Amount you must pay before your insurance will pay toward your medical care.

Coinsurance: Amount you may be required to pay for services after you pay any deductible. Coinsurance is usually a percentage of the cost for services (for example, 20%).

Copayment: Amount you may be required to pay for a medical service or prescription drug. A copayment is usually a set amount (for example, $20 for a doctor's visit).

Out-of-pocket limit: The highest amount a health plan specifies you must pay for deductibles, coinsurance and copayments. In general, the amount is per year. Not all plans have this limit. Typically, a plan with a lower monthly premium will have higher out-of-pocket costs.

MEDICARE (PART A) HOSPITAL INSURANCE: Covered Services per Benefit Period‡

Service	Benefits‡	You Pay†
Hospitalization Semi-private room and board, general nursing, and miscellaneous hospital services and supplies	First 60 days 61st day to 90th day Lifetime reserve day*	$1,408 deductible $352 per day $704 per day
Post-Hospital Skilled Nursing Facility Care In a facility approved by Medicare. You must have been admitted to a hospital for at least three days and enter the facility within 30 days after hospital discharge§ and with the same diagnosis as leaving the hospital.	First 20 days 21st to 100th day Beyond 100 days	Nothing $176 per day All costs
Home Health Care Medicare pays intermittent visits for skilled nursing care or physical therapy.	Unlimited visits as medically necessary	Nothing 20% of Medicare-approved amount for durable medical equipment
Hospice Care	Two 90-day periods and an unlimited number of 60-day periods	Copayment of up to $5 for outpatient prescription drugs and 5% of the Medicare-approved amount for inpatient respite care
Blood	Blood	In most cases, the hospital gets blood from a blood bank and you pay nothing.**

Part A covers inpatient services for a given benefit period for up to 90 days at a time. After day 90, patients have the option to use lifetime reserve days.

*Each beneficiary is granted a total of 60 lifetime reserve days. Once used, lifetime reserve days are never replaced.

† These figures are subject to change each year.

‡ A benefit period begins the day you are admitted as an inpatient and ends when you haven't received any inpatient care in a hospital or skilled nursing facility for 60 consecutive days. You can have several benefit periods per year but must pay the inpatient deductible for each benefit period.

§ Be sure that you have been *admitted* and not labeled *for observation* to the hospital in order for Medicare to pay for rehabilitation in a nursing home. Medicare and private insurance will not pay for most nursing home care. You pay for nonmedical care and most care in a nursing home unless you have a long-term care insurance policy that covers such costs.

** If the hospital has to buy blood for you, you must pay the hospital costs for the first three units of blood you get or have donors replace the blood.

Original Medicare doesn't cover (like copayments, coinsurance and deductibles). These are "gaps" in Medicare coverage.

Original Medicare doesn't pay any of your costs for a Medigap policy. If you have Original Medicare and a Medigap policy, Medicare will pay its share of the Medicare-approved amounts for covered health care costs. Then your Medigap policy pays its share.

You must have Parts A and B to get Medigap. Medigap only works with Medicare Parts A and B.

Medigap policies do not cover costs under other types of health coverage you may have.

Medigap covers one person. Spouses each need to get a policy. Once you have a Medigap policy, you should review it each year.

Medigap Costs

Cost is usually the only difference between Medigap policies with the same letter sold by different

MEDICARE (PART B) MEDICAL INSURANCE: Covered Services per Benefit Year

Service	Benefits	You Pay*
Medical Expense Physician's services, inpatient and outpatient medical services and supplies, physical and speech therapy, ambulance, chiropractic (limited), occupational therapy, durable medical equipment, prosthetic devices, second opinion before surgery, podiatrist's services, diagnostic laboratory tests, etc.	Medicare pays for medical services in or out of the hospital. Some insurance policies pay less (or nothing) for hospital outpatient medical services or services in a doctor's office.	$198 deductible* plus 20% of balance (plus any charge above the approved amount)[†]
Home Health Care Intermittent visits for skilled nursing care or physical therapy	Unlimited visits as long as medically necessary	Nothing for visits but 20% of the Medicare-approved amount for durable medical equipment. There may be limits on therapy.
Outpatient Hospital Treatment	Unlimited as long as medically necessary	A coinsurance or copayment amount that varies by service
Blood	Blood	For every unit of blood you get from a blood bank, you pay a copayment for blood processing and handling.**

Available at a monthly premium in 2020:	You Pay	If Your 2018 Yearly Income and Filing Status Is (subject to change)	
		Single	Married
	$144.60	$87,000 or less	$174,000 or less
	$202.40	$87,001-$109,000	$174,001-$218,000
	$289.20	$109,001-$136,000	$218,001-$272,000
	$376.00	$136,001-$163,000	$272,001-$326,000
	$462.70	$163,001-$499,999	$326,001-$749,999
	$491.60	$500,000 or more	$750,000 or more

*Once you have paid $198 for covered services, the Part B deductible does not apply to further covered services the rest of the year.

[†] You pay for charges greater than the amount approved by Medicare unless the doctor or supplier agrees to accept the Medicare-approved amount as the total charge for services rendered. Always ask your doctor or supplier to accept assignment. Assignment means the doctor or supplier accepts the Medicare-approved charge as full payment and can bill you only the deductible, if not already paid, plus the 20% coinsurance.

**If the provider has to buy blood for you, you must pay the provider costs for the first three units of blood you get or have donors replace the blood.

insurance companies. Although the coverage is identical for Medigap plans of the same type, premiums may vary greatly from one company or geographic area to another.

The more you pay in premiums, the less you'll pay out of pocket if you get sick, and vice versa.

More expensive policies may pay for medical care that you may or may not require. Shop around, and buy a policy that offers only what you need.

Some will pay for your Medicare premiums and deductibles. In that case, you would just pay your Medigap deductible and premium instead.

Medigap policies combined with the costs for Parts A and B can be more expensive than Medicare Advantage plans.

For guidance on how to choose a Medigap policy, go to www.medicare.gov/pubs/pdf/02110-medicare-medigap-guide.pdf or www.medicare.gov/supplements-other-insurance/how-to-compare-medigap-policies.

Find a plan by starting at www.medicare.gov /medigap-supplemental-insurance-plans.

Insurance companies use three different methods to calculate premiums: issue age, attained age and no age rating.

■ If your company uses the *issue age method* and you were 65 when you bought the policy, you will always pay the same premium the company charges people who are 65, regardless of your age.

■ If it uses the *attained age method*, the premium

All Medigap policies must follow federal and state laws designed to protect you, and policies must be clearly identified as "Medicare Supplement Insurance." Medigap insurance companies in most states can only sell you a standardized Medigap policy identified by letters A through N. Each standardized Medigap policy must offer the same basic benefits, no matter which insurance company sells it.

■ Medigap Plans C, E, F, H, I and J are no longer offered. If you are in these plans, you may keep them, but premiums are expected to rise since no new people are coming into the plans.

■ As of January 1, 2020, Medigap Plans A, B, D, G, K, L, M and N are available to all applicants.

■ In Massachusetts, Minnesota and Wisconsin, Medigap policies are standardized in a different way. Residents of these states should check with their state insurance departments for more information. **You can find contact information by going to www.medicare.gov /Contacts/#resources/sids and choosing your state.**

is based on your current age and will increase as you grow older.

■ Under the *no age rating method,* everyone pays the same premium regardless of age. The insurance company can raise your premiums only when it has approval to raise the premiums for everyone else with the same policy.

Medigap Enrollment

The best time to buy a Medigap policy is during your Medigap open enrollment period: a six-month time period customized to you. It starts in the first month that you're covered under Medicare Part B and you're 65 or older. If you delay enrolling in Part B because you have group health coverage based on your (or your spouse's) current employment, your Medigap open enrollment period won't start until you sign up for Part B.

During this period, you have guaranteed issue rights, which means you cannot be turned down or charged more for Medigap insurance due to past or present health (preexisting) conditions. After that, insurers, with certain important exceptions, may turn you down or charge you more. An example of an exception is losing health coverage because you moved.

Some states may have additional open enrollment rights under state law.

Difference Between Medigap and Medicare Advantage

A Medigap policy is different from a Medicare Advantage plan because Advantage plans are ways to get Medicare benefits while a Medigap policy only supplements the costs of your Original Medicare benefits. Medigap policies cannot be sold to those with Medicare Advantage plans. Some people decide to switch from Original Medicare to Medicare Advantage. **(See page 100.)** You always have a legal right to keep the Medigap policy after you join a Medicare Advantage plan. However, Medigap policies can't work with Medicare

Advantage plans. This means that you'll have to pay your Medigap policy premium, but the Medigap policy can't pay any deductibles, copayments, coinsurance or premiums under the Medicare Advantage plan.

It may be a good idea to continue your Medigap policy for a few months while you experience the services from your Medicare Advantage plan. If you want to drop your Medigap policy, contact your insurance company to find out how. If, in the future, you leave Medicare Advantage and switch back to Original Medicare, you might not be able to get back the same Medigap policy or, in some cases, any Medigap policy. (**See Medigap Enrollment on page 96.**)

Medicare Part D (Prescription Drugs)

The Medicare Prescription Drug Plan (Part D) offers optional drug coverage plans that may help lower prescription drug costs. Part D plans are run by private companies approved by Medicare. There are two ways to get drug coverage.

- You can buy a Part D plan to add drug coverage to Original Medicare or a Medicare Advantage plan. You will pay a separate monthly premium for your drug plan.
- You can buy a Medicare Advantage plan that includes prescription drug coverage as a benefit (as opposed to requiring the purchase of a separate plan).

Each Medicare Part D plan varies in cost and drugs covered. There used to be a coverage gap where no drug costs were paid (often called the *donut hole)*, but this was effectively closed in 2019. Starting in 2020, after you pay the deductible amount (if your plan has one) and until you reach the out-of-pocket limit ($4,020 for 2020), you will pay no more than 25% on all (brand-name and generic) covered drugs. Drug costs above the out-of-pocket limit are covered by catastrophic coverage. Catastrophic coverage requires the beneficiary to pay only a small copay or coinsurance for the rest of the coverage year.

WHERE TO FIND GUIDANCE

Medicare Compare Tool
www.medicare.gov/plan-compare

Medicare Contact Center
(800) 633-4227

Medicare Rights Center
(800) 333-4114 or www.medicarerights.org and www.medicareinteractive.org

The National Committee for Quality Assurance (NCQA)
Health Plans Report Cards
https://reportcards.ncqa.org/#/health-plans/list
List of health plans and their accreditation status

Your State Health Insurance Assistance Program
Offers local, personalized counseling
www.shiptacenter.org

National Council on Aging
www.mymedicarematters.org

Check if your income meets the level where you will pay an income-related monthly adjustment in addition to the premium. This will be deducted from your monthly Social Security benefit payment; if the amount is more than your payment, you will receive a bill.

Medicare Part D Enrollment

Enrollment dates are determined by your age and whether you are still working and have coverage under another plan.

Age 65. When turning 65, you can enroll during the period three months before and after the month of your 65th birthday.

Late enrollment penalty. If you do not select a Medicare prescription drug plan when you are first eligible and do not have other prescription drug coverage at least as good (called *creditable coverage)* as Medicare, you may have to pay an ongoing penalty if you select a plan at a later date.

If you or your spouse are still working at age 65. If you're covered under an employer or union plan and your current plan has determined that your drug coverage is creditable coverage, you can keep your current plan as long as it is still offered. Once the employer or union no longer offers its drug plan, you will not have to pay a late enrollment penalty as long as you join a Medicare drug plan within 63 days after the coverage ends.

Open enrollment. Once you are enrolled in a Part D plan, open enrollment is each year during the period from October 15 through December 7, with coverage to begin on January 1 of the following year. Each year during this period, even if you are satisfied with your plan, review your choices. Plans can change costs and benefits, so you might want to switch to another Part D plan. Verify that your medications are still covered.

If you do not currently take a lot of prescriptions, consider joining a drug plan that has the lowest premium.

Medicare Advantage (Part C)

This type of coverage is an alternative to Original Medicare. Medicare Advantage plans, offered by private insurers approved by Medicare, provide extra benefits and potentially lower copayments than Original Medicare. Most Medicare Advantage plans also cover the cost for prescription drugs (Part D). However, you may be limited to specific doctors and hospitals that belong to the plan. Before signing up, make sure your doctor and other providers are in the network.

About one-third of all Medicare beneficiaries (22 million people) are enrolled in Medicare Advantage plans, according to an analysis by the Kaiser Family Foundation. The Congressional Budget Office (CBO) projects that the share of beneficiaries enrolled in Medicare Advantage plans will rise to about 47% by 2029.

Benefits Covered

Medicare Advantage coverage includes all of the services provided under Medicare Parts A and B, except hospice care. Medicare Advantage plans may include some extra benefits like vision, hearing or dental coverage. Some Medicare Advantage plans may offer extra nonmedical benefits for people with chronic illness, including home safety modifications, grocery delivery, transportation for nonmedical needs and pest control. All Medicare Advantage plans cover emergency and urgent care. Read the policies carefully so you understand what is covered and what is excluded.

Costs

You will have to pay your monthly Medicare Part B premium to Medicare. Each month, Medicare pays a fixed amount for your coverage to the insurer offering your Medicare Advantage plan. In addition, you might have to pay a monthly premium to your Medicare Advantage plan for the extra benefits that it offers. Review your plan carefully for out-of-pocket costs. Most plans have an annual out-of-pocket limit.

Even with a Medicare Advantage plan, the hospital coverage that would be categorized as Part A coverage is still premium-free. But usually you will pay the Part B premium and a Medicare Advantage premium to the private insurer.

Medicare Advantage Networks

The main types of Medicare Advantage plans are preferred provider organizations (PPOs) and health maintenance organizations (HMOs).

Medicare Advantage PPOs

The costs are based on a network of health care providers that have contracted with an insurance company to provide care at an agreed-upon rate. In a PPO, you pay less if you use doctors, hospitals and other health care providers that belong to the plan's network. You're not restricted to certain doctors or hospitals, but you pay more if you use care outside of the network (except emergency care). In general, you don't need a referral to see a specialist.

Medicare Advantage HMOs

In an HMO, health care providers are banded into a network. You are assigned a primary care physician (some plans may use a nurse practitioner working with a physician) who coordinates your health care through this network. The primary care physician takes care of your routine medical needs. To see a specialist, you must first get a referral from the primary care physician (who in turn may need to gain approval from an HMO administrator). If you get health care outside the plan's network, except for emergency care, you may have to pay the full cost.

HMOs operate within a defined service area. If you expect to spend a lot of time away from home, check with the HMO of your choice to see if they have reciprocal care arrangements with an HMO in the area in which you will be spending substantial time.

It is important to note that there is no standard HMO. Plans vary widely in terms of services offered, the quality of those services and amounts charged. Enrollment in an HMO may provide access to a broader array of health services at an overall lower cost. HMOs are in a period of change; some may curtail their service areas and/or reduce their benefits.

Before you join an HMO, do your homework. Focus on its reputation for promptly providing needed services regardless of the cost involved. An HMO's service ethic is ultimately the most decisive factor in judging its appropriateness for you. Health care is more than a financial decision.

Medicare Advantage Enrollment

Open enrollment for Medicare Advantage is the same as Original Medicare and runs October 15 to December 7. To join a Medicare Advantage plan, you must have Medicare Part A and Part B. During the open enrollment period, you can:

- Switch from Original Medicare to Medicare Advantage, or vice versa.
- Switch from one Medicare Advantage plan to another
- Switch from one Part D plan to another.

From January 1 to March 31, Medicare Advantage enrollees can:

- Switch to a new Medicare Advantage plan
- Return to Original Medicare.

Once You're Enrolled

If you want to switch between Medicare Advantage plans, you can do so between January 1 and March 31 and October 15 and December 7.

Following are some reasons you might consider switching.

- You moved to a new geographic region and your plan only covered doctors in a certain region.
- The plan may no longer be a good fit for your health needs based on changes made during the past year.
- Your doctors are not covered in the network. Your plan can change the providers in your network at any time. Providers can decide to join or leave the network at any time.
- Your prescription drug is not covered.

During the fall, you should receive notices of these changes.

Differences Between Medicare Advantage and Original Medicare

One isn't better than the other. Here are some things to consider.

Your doctors. If you have relationships with doctors already in place and sticking with them is important to you, then the availability of those doctors within a plan will be a key consideration.

Networks. Are you comfortable seeking care only at specified facilities? If you move and your plan is based on a regional network, you will have to enroll in a new Medicare Advantage program. Being limited to a network can cause a problem if you travel often. Original Medicare covers any doctor and hospital that has agreed to be paid at Medicare rates.

Referrals to specialists. Each Medicare Advantage plan has different rules for how services are provided—for example, whether a beneficiary needs a referral to see a specialist (which means paying for two doctor visits). These rules can change each year. Original Medicare doesn't require a referral.

Premiums. Original Medicare plus a Medigap policy will have a predictable premium and low deductible. Medicare Advantage plans have low or no premiums with a higher deductible, so your monthly expenses could spike if you need medical care.

Out-of-pocket limit and risk. Original Medicare has no yearly limit on what you pay out of pocket, unless you have a Medigap policy. Medicare Advantage plans have a yearly limit on what you pay out of pocket for Medicare Part A- and Part B-covered services, and it varies by plan. Once you reach your plan's limit, you'll pay nothing for Part A- and Part B-covered services for the rest of the year. Sometimes you know what kind of medical care you need and how often you need it. You can use that knowledge to choose a plan. But health changes—and in turn risk to your finances—can happen at any time.

Switching Between Medicare Advantage and Original Medicare

It can be tricky to go back and forth.

From Advantage to Original

Medicare Advantage members can switch to Original Medicare and a Part D drug plan between January 1 and March 31. The main reasons to make a switch are changes in coverage for drugs, doctors and/or specialists and if you are going to be traveling a lot or living in multiple locations. Original Medicare places fewer limits on where you can get health care.

It's hard for some people to go back to Original Medicare because Medigap plans can exclude people with preexisting conditions. **(See page 96.)** There are some situations in which an insurance company can't refuse to sell you a Medigap policy even if you have health problems. For example:

- If you join Medicare Advantage when you are first eligible and decide that you don't like the plan, you have a 12-month time frame in which you can switch back to Original Medicare, and Medigap insurers cannot deny your application.

- If you move within your state or to another state and the Medicare Advantage plan doesn't serve that area, you can switch to Original Medicare. You must apply within 63 days of losing your coverage.

From Original to Advantage

If you join a Medicare Advantage plan, your Medigap policy won't work. This means it won't pay any deductibles, copayments or other cost-sharing expenses under your Original Medicare plan. You have a legal right to keep the Medigap policy, although you might want to drop it. **(See page 96.)**

Health Savings Accounts

Health savings accounts (HSAs) allow people enrolled in high-deductible health plans (HDHPs) to deposit pretax dollars for health expenses and to receive a tax deduction for contributions up until the age of 65 or until they enroll in Medicare.

Contributing and Investing

You must have HDHP coverage when you contribute to an HSA. If you enroll in Medicare, you are no longer eligible to contribute to an

HSA. If you qualify for premium-free Part A, your coverage will go back (retroactively) up to six months from when you sign up. So you should stop making contributions to your HSA six months before you enroll in Part A and Part B (or apply for Social Security benefits, if you want to collect retirement benefits before you stop working).

IRS changes the definition of *high deductible* each year. In 2020, the minimum annual deductible is $1,400 for self-only HDHP coverage and $2,800 for family HDHP coverage.

The 2020 annual HSA contribution limit is $3,550 for individuals with self-only HDHP coverage and $7,100 for individuals with family HDHP coverage. The HSA catch-up contribution limit (for HSA-eligible individuals age 55 or older) is $1,000 for 2020.

How much you're able to contribute to an HSA is a personal decision. Ask yourself: Do you have enough cash to cover your deductible and your annual out-of-pocket maximum this year? If you need to use your HSA contributions for current medical expenses, focus on building up that short-term savings cushion.

If you have a long time horizon and you have enough short-term savings to cover your current medical expenses, it is important to invest your HSA funds the same way you would with a retirement plan.

HSA Withdrawals in Retirement

You do not have to have HDHP coverage when you make withdrawals. HSA withdrawals can pay for medical expenses for your spouse and your dependents, even if they do not have HDHP coverage. Make sure you save all your related receipts in case you are ever audited. Similar to a tax audit, you will need proof of what you purchased using your account.

What You Can Pay for Tax-Free

Withdrawing money from an HSA is tax-free for the cost of medical care and drugs as well as premiums for Part B and Part D prescription-drug coverage (but not supplemental/Medigap policy premiums). If you have retiree employer-sponsored health coverage, an HSA can also be used to pay your share of those costs. You can use a limited amount (based on your age and with slight annual increases) to pay for certain long-term care insurance premiums.

If you withdraw for something other than the tax-free options, your withdrawals will be treated as ordinary income (10% after age 65 and 20% before age 65).

There is no requirement to begin withdrawing funds at a certain age.

Designate a Beneficiary for Your HSA

If your spouse is the designated beneficiary, your spouse can take over the HSA. If someone other than your spouse is the beneficiary, the account ceases to function as an HSA after your death.

WHAT MEDICARE COVERS AND ANNUAL HEALTH CARE COSTS

Instead of thinking of health care costs in retirement as a total amount (estimated to be hundreds of thousands of dollars), budget your health care costs as an annual expense. Your annual health care costs are a combination of predictable monthly premiums that can be budgeted for and less predictable expenses (out of pocket) that can be managed from savings. The good news is that the predictable monthly premium payments make up the bulk of annual health care costs in retirement. According to a T. Rowe Price analysis, premiums with prescription drug coverage account for nearly 75% of annual health care costs for the majority of retirees, regardless of the type of Medicare coverage they have.

Turning 65 and Still Working

If you're still working and covered by your employer's plan, you have more options to consider and different dates to keep track of. Keep in mind that Medicare doesn't know you are still working and you may get mail that is written for people who are not working. When you turn 65, you will become eligible for Medicare, but that doesn't mean you have to enroll right away.

Before you turn 65, figure out the size of your employer.

- If you work for an employer that has fewer than 20 employees, you usually need to sign up for Medicare at age 65 (Original or Advantage) because the rules say Medicare will be your primary insurance. The enrollment period begins three months before the month you turn 65 and ends three months after your birthday month.

- If you work for an employer that has 20 or more employees, you have more options. Your employer-based insurance will be your primary insurance.
  - You can have your employer coverage only, or
  - You can have your employer coverage and Medicare (Part A only or Parts A and B).

Medicare (if you sign up) becomes your secondary insurer, so it might pay for some of the costs that your employer insurance doesn't cover. You may want to compare what your out-of-pocket costs will be under each option to help you decide. Keep in mind that you would pay premiums on your employer coverage and Part B if you enroll. If your employer plan (which pays primary) pays the health care provider equal to or more than what Medicare would pay, then Medicare (as secondary) wouldn't pay at all.

FAQs: If You Are Still Working When You Turn 65 and Your Employer Has at Least 20 Full-Time Employees and Offers Health Insurance Coverage

1. *Do I need to enroll in Medicare when I turn 65 if I'm still working and covered under my employer plan?*

A: Not for Parts A and B, unless your employer has fewer than 20 employees. That said, the Centers for Medicare and Medicaid Services (CMS) says most people should enroll in Medicare Part A when they turn 65 even if they have employer health insurance. This is because most people paid Medicare taxes while they worked and therefore do not pay a monthly premium for Part A.

People who may want to consider delaying Medicare Part A include those who contribute to a health savings account (HSA) and those who have to pay a premium for Part A because they didn't work enough to qualify for premium-free Part A.

If you were covered for medical insurance by your employer while working and will still be covered in retirement, signing up for Medicare Part B insurance may not be necessary—and then you don't have to pay the monthly premium.

The answer also is no for Part D, as long as the employer prescription drug plan is creditable (i.e., it pays at least as much as Medicare would).

2. *How do I know if my employer prescription drug coverage is creditable?*

A: Each year you are eligible for Part D, your insurance plan should send you a letter before October 15 telling you whether or not the employer's coverage is creditable. October 15 is the start of the open enrollment period for Part D.

3. *My spouse is turning 65 and is covered under my plan. Can he or she stay on my plan, or does my spouse have to enroll in Medicare?*

A: It depends on the eligibility rules of your plan. Spouses may stay on employer plans as long as the plan eligibility allows. If your plan says spouses can stay on the plan, they do not need to enroll in Medicare as long as they are on the employer plan. If your spouse is collecting Social Security, he or she would need to enroll in Medicare. Talk to your employee benefits administrator.

4. *I enrolled in Social Security before I turned 65 and am still working. What do I do if I don't want Medicare at age 65?*

A: You will automatically be enrolled in Medicare Part A at no cost to you (see Question 1 about Part A). You need to contact Social Security to say you want to decline Medicare Part B.

5. *What do I do if I have a high-deductible health plan (HDHP) and still want to contribute to my HSA?*

A: Do not sign up for Medicare, not even Part A. Do not sign up for Social Security because you will be automatically signed up for Part A. The Internal Revenue Service (IRS) does not allow contributing to an HSA while being covered under any part of Medicare. You should stop making HSA contributions six months before you do sign up for Medicare.

If you enrolled in Social Security before you turned 65, then you will automatically be enrolled in Medicare when you turn 65. You need to stop HSA contributions the month before you turn 65.

6. *I delayed Medicare enrollment because I'm still working. What do I do when I'm ready to retire?*

A: Apply for Medicare three months before your employer coverage will end. The end date is typically the last day of the month in which you retired, but plans vary, so check with your benefits administrator. If you choose Original Medicare, mark your calendar to apply for a Medigap plan right away once you have Part B coverage.

7. *Will I be penalized for delaying Medicare enrollment?*

A: No, as long as you sign up for Medicare within eight months after the date you stop working or lose coverage, whichever comes first. Mark your calendar.

HOW MEDICARE WORKS WITH OTHER INSURANCE

Coordination-of-benefits rules decide whether Medicare or other insurance pays first.

- The insurance that pays first (primary payer) pays what it owes on your bills up to the limits of its coverage.

- The one that pays second (secondary payer) only pays if there are costs the primary insurer didn't cover.

- The secondary payer (which may be Medicare) may not pay all the uncovered costs. Typically, you will be billed at that point.

For many people (those with insurance through an employer with 20-plus employees), employer health insurance will be the primary payer and Medicare will be the secondary payer. As secondary payer, Medicare will only pay your bill if your primary insurance pays less than the amount Medicare would have paid if it were the primary payer. Employer health coverage typically covers more of the cost than Medicare covers, which would result in Medicare making no payment. This means that you are not likely to see any cost savings from having Medicare in addition to your employer plan.

Affordable Care Act (ACA)

This section is intended for people who:

- Do not have Medicare or Medicaid
- Are not eligible for employer-sponsored coverage
- Are offered employer-sponsored coverage that is unaffordable or does not meet minimum standards required by the Affordable Care Act (ACA).

Because purchasing health coverage has historically been a private decision, millions of Americans remain uninsured each year, usually by choice or because health insurance is unaffordable for them. In an effort to address and minimize this insurance gap, the ACA (also known as ObamaCare) was passed in 2010 with the intent of making health care affordable and accessible for all people. ACA-compliant plans must cover treatment for preexisting medical conditions.

ACA is still the current law, but there is controversy about what ACA was intended to do, whether it was effectively designed and if it has achieved its goals. Parts of the law have and may continue to change.

Most people primarily obtain health insurance through employer-sponsored group health plans. For those who don't, another option is to purchase an individual policy directly from an insurance company or through a marketplace (public exchange) regulated by ACA.

ACA coverage can be purchased at the marketplace website, www.healthcare.gov, where you can shop for health insurance plans that have been approved for sale by the state or federal government. The open enrollment period generally begins in November of the calendar year before coverage begins. The length of the open enrollment period and the date it closes change each year. **Go to www.healthcare.gov to apply and learn about your options.**

Insurers and premiums will vary in each state. Before signing up for a policy, make sure your doctors, hospitals and other providers are covered in the plan. Going outside the plan can be expensive.

As you near age 65 and are enrolling in Medicare, don't forget to notify your marketplace plan that you will be dropping coverage. Coordinate the end date of your plan with the effective date of your Medicare enrollment.

Because many of its aspects (enhancing access and affordability) have high costs associated with them, ACA was designed to include taxes, including the individual shared responsibility penalty (individual mandate). In 2019, the federal individual mandate fee no longer applies. But some states have passed individual mandates that require residents to have health insurance or pay a state tax penalty.

If you currently have a policy, you will automatically be reenrolled in your current plan unless you take action. This could cost money. The premiums charged by your current account could increase, and new plans may be available. Keep up to date since there may be changes to ACA.

You can still buy coverage directly from insurers outside the marketplace. They may have lower premiums. Private exchanges are separate and distinct from ACA. You can buy private insurance from a health insurance agent. **See www.eHealthInsurance.com.**

U.S. Supreme Court cases have challenged the constitutionality of various funding elements, and Congress has made several attempts to abolish or delay some of these taxes. As these funding mechanisms are changed or eliminated, questions remain about whether ACA will be gradually dismantled. A 2018 Michigan Retirement Research Center study found that older workers aren't retiring sooner (whether they are financially ready or not) as a result of ACA marketplace alternatives to employer-based health insurance. One reason for this could be because of the uncertainty surrounding the law.

Medicaid

Medicaid is a program of assistance to those of any age who need medical services they cannot afford.

Retiree Health Coverage

When you are planning to retire, find out if your employer offers retiree health care coverage. Many employers do not offer retiree health coverage. Some do if you retire before you are eligible for Medicare. Employers control the retiree coverage they offer. Employers aren't required to provide retiree coverage, and they can change benefits or premiums or cancel coverage.

If your employer offers retiree health coverage, here are some steps to take before you retire.

- Find out the premiums and benefits of the retiree coverage, including whether it includes coverage for your spouse (if you're married) and whether the plan limits how much it will pay for health care. Depending on how generous the retiree coverage is, you may want to talk to your State Health Insurance Assistance Program (SHIP) for advice about whether to buy a Medigap policy.

- Plan ahead for Medicare Part A and Part B enrollment. Retiree coverage isn't based on current employment in terms of Medicare enrollment. This means that when you become eligible for Medicare (during your initial enrollment period), even if you have retiree coverage, you will need to enroll in both Medicare Part A and Part B. There are two reasons for this.

  - When you have retiree coverage, Medicare pays first (primary) and your employer/union pays next (secondary). **(See box on page 103.)**

  - If you enroll after your initial enrollment period passes, you may have a late enrollment penalty that requires you to pay a higher premium in perpetuity. **(See enrollment information on page 92.)**

- Find out what effect your continued coverage as a retiree will have on both your health coverage and your spouse's health coverage. If you're not sure how your retiree coverage works with Medicare, call your plan's benefits administrator to ask how the plan pays when you have Original Medicare and/or Medicare Advantage.

  - In some cases, joining a Medicare Advantage plan might cause you to lose your employer or union coverage for yourself, your spouse and your dependents, and you may not be able to get it back. In other cases, you may still be able to use your employer or union coverage along with a Medicare Advantage plan. Your employer or union may also sponsor and offer a Medicare Advantage retiree health plan.

There are income and net worth limits for Medicaid eligibility. These limits differ from state to state. Essentially, a Medicaid recipient and spouse may have income up to a certain amount and also retain assets up to a certain amount, including one's home, and be eligible for Medicaid. Medicaid rules are very complicated. Check with your attorney, senior center or local government office of aging for specific details. Check now so you're prepared when and if you need Medicaid in the future.

Because Medicare does not cover long-term nursing home nonmedical care, which can be quite costly, Medicaid is often the only option for those who find they need such care.

It is important to keep in mind that you are not expected to exhaust your life savings, go into debt or sell your home before receiving Medicaid. A lien may be placed on your home to reimburse the state for your expenses.

Long-Term Care Insurance

Medicare, Medigap and Medicare Advantage do not cover nonmedical at-home care or the full costs of nursing home expenses.

Here's some data to consider. Someone turning 65 today has almost a 70% chance of needing some type of long-term care either at home or in a facility, according to the Department of Health and Human Services (HHS). One-third of today's 65-year-olds may never need long-term care support, but 20% will need it for longer than five years. A survey by Genworth reported that the average nursing home costs $89,000 per year for semiprivate rooms and $100,000 for private rooms, and these costs can be considerably more in certain areas. Most people don't have long claim periods. The Center for Retirement Research found that men who need nursing home care will spend less than 11 months in care, on average, while women will spend about 17 months.

There are long-term care policies that help protect assets that otherwise might have to be

MEDICARE VS. MEDICAID

- Medicare exists to provide health coverage for qualified people age 65 and older who have paid Medicare payroll taxes and are not enrolled in a different health insurance plan. Disabled individuals who have received Social Security Disability Insurance (SSDI) benefits for more than 24 months are also eligible for Medicare.

- Medicaid is jointly funded by federal and state governments and offers health coverage to specific segments of the population at or near the poverty level. Each state determines the eligibility rules that apply to residents of that state.

- If you qualify for a government program like Medicare or Medicaid, then you don't need to purchase marketplace coverage.

- If you enroll in a government program like Medicare or Medicaid, then you are covered for the individual mandate.

liquidated in order to pay the high costs of nursing home care. But long-term care insurance premiums have been rising sharply while benefits have been cut back. Insurance companies consider your current health conditions when determining your eligibility and premiums. It costs less to buy coverage when you are younger. The average age of people buying long-term care insurance today is about 60.

Some states allow state income deductions or credits for premiums. These vary from state to state. Long-term care premiums can now be paid through tax-advantaged HSAs. (**See page 100.**)

Things to know before you buy long-term care insurance.

- The *elimination period* is the amount of time that must pass after you start receiving care before the policy starts paying for your care. Most policies allow you to choose an elimination period of 30, 60 or 90 days, during which you must cover the cost of any services you receive.

- Many long-term care insurance policies have limits on how long or how much they will pay. Some policies will pay the costs of your long-term care for two to five years.

- Don't buy more insurance than you think you may need. You may have enough income to pay a portion of your care costs, and you may only need a small policy for the remainder.

- One option is to buy a scaled-back policy that would pay enough benefits to cover a short stay in a facility or a few hours of home care a day.

- If you want to remain at home and have family members who can provide some care, for example, you may want to buy a policy with a relatively low benefit level. The policy could provide enough to cover the cost of an aide for two to three hours a day to give family caregivers a break.

- Look carefully at each policy. There is no one-size-fits-all policy.

- Make sure the premiums are well within your budget indefinitely. Consider your retirement income sources and if you will be living on a fixed income. This can be especially hard to do because premium increases are common.

- If you choose a policy that only pays for room and board in a facility, plan for other expenses such as supplies, medications, linens, and other items and services that your policy may not cover.

Most people buy long-term care insurance directly from an insurance agent, a financial planner or a broker. The best way to find out which insurance companies offer long-term care coverage in your state is to contact your state's Department of Insurance.

Learn more at:

- **U.S. Department of Health & Human Services—www.longtermcare.gov**
- **A Shopper's Guide to Long-Term Care Insurance —www.naic.org/documents /prod_serv_consumer_ltc_lp.pdf.**

Be careful: The policies are very complicated. Don't be pressured into buying one. It might not be a good deal for everyone. (**See Chapter 15 on caregiving.**)

Health Records

Maintain your own medical records by writing down relevant facts about your health, your test results, and a list of current medications, dosages and supplements. List any symptoms you may be experiencing. Keep a copy of your living will. (**See Chapter 5.**) Collect as much information as you can about the health history of your family, and share it with your doctor.

The U.S. Surgeon General Family History has an initiative to raise public awareness of the importance of knowing your family health history. Tracing the illnesses suffered by your parents, grandparents and other blood relatives can help your doctor predict the disorders for which you may be at risk and help you take action to keep you and your family healthy. *My Family Health Portrait* is a website that helps you create a printable chart of your family health history. **Go to www.genome .gov/For-Patients-and-Families/Family-Health -History.**

Steps for an Appeal

Have you been denied a claim for a service you received? If so, you have the right to appeal.

Depending on the type of coverage you have, the appeal process will vary. The following are steps to take.

- Document everything. As you proceed, keep records of all interactions with your provider, doctor or hospital, including authorizations and specialist referrals. Document every call, conversation or email. Note the name of any person you communicate with, the date and time of your communication, and what you talked about. Keep a copy of all documents that you send.

- If your medical condition requires prompt attention, pay the bill under protest. Then proceed with your appeal.
- Be strong but civil. Even though you may be upset, you can get your point across better by being courteous and rational.
- **For assistance, contact your local State Health Insurance Assistance Program (SHIP) at www.shiptacenter.org or (877) 839-2675.**

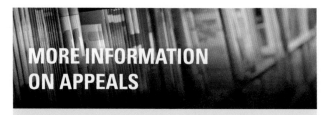

MORE INFORMATION ON APPEALS

Original Medicare

Check www.medicare.gov/appeals.

Medicare & You at www.medicare.gov /pubs/pdf/10050-medicare-and-you.pdf.

Medicare Advantage Appeals

The Medicare Advantage appeals process can vary from plan to plan. If you go out of network or fail to get preauthorization for a procedure, you will get billed. Know the rules for your coverage. If you didn't follow the rules for staying in network or getting preapproval for a procedure, you will get billed. You likely cannot appeal the claim denial.

Medicare Prescription Drug Appeals

The process for Medicare prescription drug appeals can vary from plan to plan.

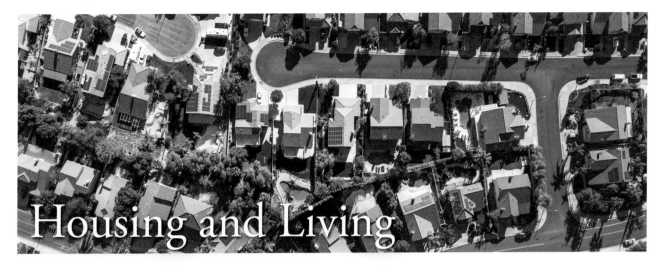

Housing and Living

"Home is any four walls that enclose the right person." —Helen Rowland

Where Will You Live?

When people start looking into where they might settle down in retirement, there are three questions that stand out.

- Where will I live when I'm retired?
- Should I move or stay here?
- If I move, where should I go?

They are very serious questions. The right decision could determine how comfortable, happy and secure retirement will be. It is not too early to think about all of this, even if retirement is still ten years in the future. Picture yourself retired, free of work-related responsibilities and living where you would be happiest in retirement. Remember: Where you live in retirement will be a critical factor in what you do for the extra income you might need, for personal relationships, for leisure activities, for health and comfort, etc.

What you choose will depend upon your relationships, family ties, circumstances, needs and preferences. Some factors are in your control, and some are not. Your health may dictate that you should move to a milder climate. Your plans for leisure activities may make you move closer to nature or keep you close to the cultural offerings of

a larger city or college town. This chapter will give you an idea of your options and what factors come into play. Explore all your options.

Retirement Living and Longevity

Today, we tend to live longer and have healthier, more active lifestyles than previous generations, potentially giving us 20 years or more of living where and how we want to. This chapter focuses on your options in those early years. It's different for everyone but, for those who live to around age 80, health and physical mobility have a bigger impact on where and how we live and what kind of care we need. **For information on home care and nursing homes, see Chapter 15.**

Many Think About Moving

The majority of those retiring say that they have given some thought to relocating. However, most stay close to where they are.

In a study by Age Wave, nearly two-thirds of retirees have moved or plan to move, either within the same community or into homes in other cities and states. Among other things, wanting to lower home expenses; encountering health challenges, divorce or widowhood; and dealing with an empty nest can all be triggers for moving in retirement. However, retirees report wanting to be closer to family as a top reason for moving.

Studies indicate that only 20% to 25% of those who retire move away from their home communities within the first few years of retirement. Most who move stay in the same state. Perhaps no more than 5% move to other states and other parts of the country.

Of the 75% to 80% who remain in their home communities, a substantial number move to smaller homes or apartments.

Most Stay Put

Surveys of older adults have consistently found that most people want to stay in their homes and communities. Why do most people stay where they are? It's not simply inertia. Many people have an emotional connection to the home and value the memories made there. They want to remain near friends and neighbors, family and grandchildren; stay in clubs and organizations with people they know; do business with banks and stores they are accustomed to, etc. If they want to continue to work, it's convenient to stay close to former workplaces or remain in close contact with their professional network. In a nutshell, they want to continue living as much as possible as they did before retirement. Some people may stay put because moving is unaffordable.

Some people who have paid off a mortgage make it a short-term savings goal to update the home with new technology and other features that can help accommodate the aging process, with the goal of continuing to live independently as long as possible.

Where You Live Now

In thinking about where you will live in retirement, it is a good idea to begin by thinking about where you are living now.

- Why did you choose your present home?
- What are its advantages?
- What are its disadvantages?
- Did you make sacrifices in order to be convenient to your job or, perhaps, your spouse's job?
- Did you live there to be near schools, a consideration that is no longer an advantage now that children are grown?
- Does your present home have space you no longer need, perhaps a larger yard for children?

There is a good test of how happy and well-adjusted a retiree will be in a new retirement home: How happy are you in your present community?

If you are happy and active in your area, enjoying its advantages and helping to serve its needs, there is almost no doubt that you can be as happy and adjusted in a new home.

If you have never become a part of your neighborhood, because you are too busy or just not interested, don't expect changes if you relocate.

Downsizing or Upsizing

Think of what you might gain—or give up—by moving into a smaller home requiring less care, inside and outdoors, and costing less for utilities and perhaps for taxes. In some areas of the country where housing costs are spiking, a condo may cost more than you would net from the sale of your house. If you do have equity tied up in a home, selling may help add to your savings for retirement.

Whether you are moving to a smaller home or out of state, this could be the time to downsize some of your belongings, distribute some personal treasures to family members or friends, or donate some items to charity.

Half of retirees didn't downsize in their last move, according to a survey by Agewave. In fact, one-third upsized into a larger home. Retirees say a top reason to upsize is to have a home that is large and comfortable enough for family members to visit and stay with them. Retirees with children and grandchildren often find their homes becoming the place for family to gather, especially during holidays or vacations. Another reason to keep a larger home or move to one is so that family members can move in, if needed. According to the Agewave survey, 16% of retirees had a "boomerang" adult child who had moved back home.

Living With Relatives

Health factors may combine with economic ones to make living with children or relatives a necessity. It's hard to give up independence. On the plus side, you may avoid the sense of isolation that may come with living alone.

No matter how close your relationship may be, combining two independent family units changes the dynamics of the family and may cause stress for everyone. A few issues are privacy, routines, activity schedules, home expenses, pets, personal boundaries and doing things that bother other family members. It will require tact, maturity and considerable caring on the part of everyone involved to ensure that relationships in the household stay strong.

There should be an understanding about roles in the family. Where possible, a private living room, bedroom and bath facilities will enable you to have more independence. Talk about the costs and time line of any necessary safety upgrades. Ideally, maintain a schedule independent of the activities of the family, and cultivate friendships and interests apart from those at home.

Moving Closer to Family or Friends

Being closer to family or friends is the most common reason people move. The wide separation of families and friends in our society is in sharp contrast to well-rooted, close-knit families and communities abroad. Perhaps seeking to restart ties as retirement approaches, many Americans consider moving closer to children, grandchildren, other relatives or good friends who have moved away.

But should you? There are many factors to be considered in addition to a natural desire to be closer to family and friends. It's not enough to say, "It would be good to be near the kids."

Their way of life may not be yours. Their friends might not become your friends. If they should decide to seek better job opportunities elsewhere, you might be left behind, lonelier than ever.

Cost of living is another factor. Some retirees relocate near children who live in fast-growing cities where the housing market is soaring and then find themselves taking on a mortgage in retirement or using savings set aside for another purpose to afford housing.

Experts suggest you start planning where you will live in retirement about ten years before you hope to retire. This gives you time to be methodical and thoughtful about your research as well as self-aware of what will make you happy. Talk openly with your loved ones. Be flexible too, because life happens—Some factors that life throws at you are out of your control.

Moving is physically and psychologically difficult, and it can be an expensive drain on retirement resources. Carefully think it through rather than making a snap judgment because you enjoyed a place on vacation or because it offers sunshine right after you've been through a harsh winter. Being cautious and sure of your decision may prevent you from being sorry after it's too late.

Relocation Considerations

According to a United Van Lines study, relocating retirees tended to look for affordable states with temperate climates where they can participate in outdoor activities.

Here are some things to consider.

- **Climate, geography and scenery:** No place offers a perfect year-round climate. It's a good idea to visit a location you're interested in at different times of the year—and stay long enough (perhaps in a short-term rental) to recognize the flaws along with the advantages.

Are there safe places to walk both indoors and outdoors? Summer vacations could be a start, but take time to sample other seasons.

- **Health advantages and facilities:** Many who relocate do so for health reasons. Respiratory, coronary and rheumatic conditions can be relieved by settling in the right place or can be aggravated by a wrong choice. When making a decision about moving, consult your doctor. And wherever you go, check on the availability of doctors, hospitals and clinics. Don't take for granted that emergency help will be available. Medicare Advantage plans that are based on regional networks don't transfer at all. You'll have to enroll again if you move far enough to be out of the network service area. **Check www.medicare.gov/plan-compare to find a new plan before you move.**

- **Housing-related expenses:** Check the housing market in any area in which you want to relocate. Research whether it makes sense to rent initially or buy. Possible expenses include rent or mortgage payments, property taxes, insurance, utilities, homeowners association fees, repair and maintenance.

- **Economics:** Check the cost of living and compare it with your current budget. It's a good idea to check local ads and websites to learn about consumer prices, real estate and business activities. If you want to augment your income in retirement, are there job opportunities? You might want to check with the Chamber of Commerce or a senior citizen agency. Remember, if you save money on clothing, heating and housing costs in Sun Belt areas, the savings may be partially offset by air conditioning costs during most of the year. Ask about any leisure and association fees.

- **Social and spiritual opportunities:** The biggest challenge some retirees face is reestablishing a community of friends when they move, which is why many are drawn to places with large numbers of older adults. Make sure that

you can continue to enjoy the kind of social and spiritual life you have had before. The same advice goes for recreational and sports possibilities and for hobbies. The friendship you find in social, spiritual, recreational, sports and hobby groups is important to your happiness in a new home.

- **Cultural and intellectual advantages:** Some people will want a community that offers cultural and intellectual opportunities. College towns often provide features like medical facilities, libraries, cultural organizations, concerts, sporting events and art galleries. Many schools allow retirees to audit classes for free, and some retirees volunteer at a college.

- **Location and accessibility:** Shopping centers, restaurants, libraries, theaters, post offices and other everyday facilities are easily accessible almost everywhere now. Certainly you'll have no problems if you have a car. Still, be sure to check. Also, don't forget to look into the accessibility of airports offering adequate flight service, and estimate the cost of traveling to the places you hope to go. Is there train and bus service?

- **Personal relationships:** If you have no friends or relatives in the place you'd like to make your retirement home, visit enough times to be sure the residents are friendly. Almost always they will be, but outsiders may find it hard to break through barriers in a few places. The lack of quick friendliness and acceptance in a community can create additional strain at a time when tearing up roots in one place and trying to set them in another is hard enough.

- **Crime:** Check local news sites to get a sampling of the good and bad news in the area. To get accurate crime statistics, contact the local police precinct in a particular neighborhood. This will give you better results than statistics for an entire city or state. If you're concerned about crime, then gated community options may be best for you.

- **Legal considerations:** If you move out of state, you should have your will reviewed. You might need to draw up a new will in your new home state since laws can differ from state to state. If you are going to live in two states, check that your will, power of attorney and durable power of attorney for health care follow the rules in both states.
- **Taxes:** If moving to another state, county or municipality, find out what your total tax burden will be. Review all income taxes, sales taxes, property taxes, and estate and inheritance taxes. Some states will charge income tax on Social Security and pension benefits. Some states have programs that give senior or disabled homeowners a break. States often adjust their tax systems, so be sure to regularly check this information.

   For more information on taxes, go to:
- **Retirement Living Information Center, www.retirementliving.com/taxes-by-state**
- **Kiplinger's State-by-State Guide to Taxes on Retirees www.Kiplinger.com/links /retireetaxmap.**

TAXES AND THE SALE OF YOUR HOME

When you sell your primary residence, you can deduct up to $250,000 in profit if you're single and up to $500,000 if you're married. The exclusion can be used more than once. The home or apartment must be the primary residence of at least one spouse for at least two of the past five years. A surviving spouse can sell a home that was jointly owned within two years of a spouse passing away and still file for the $500,000 capital-gains exclusion. If you sell your primary home, be aware that high profit sales can trigger the special 3.8% Medicare tax, which will be assessed if the seller has an adjusted gross income of $200,000 for singles and $250,000 for couples. On sales of second homes, the Medicare tax can hit the entire gain.

Types of Living Arrangements

Senior housing and independent living arrangements are broadening to meet the demands of Baby Boomers who aren't as interested in retirement communities designed for previous generations. Continuing care retirement communities—where a resident can transition from independent living to assisted living to intensive nursing care all in one place, often with the requirement of a hefty entrance fee and ongoing monthly fees—may still be the best option for some people. Some other arrangements that are more organically formed and can be intergenerational may be especially appealing to people who are single.

- **Shared housing** means living with unrelated adults like on the TV show *Golden Girls*. **See www.nationalsharedhousing.org.**
- **Co-housing communities** are homes located around shared spaces, where neighbors commit to interacting for everyone's mutual benefit. Typically, there is a common house that may include a large kitchen and dining area, laundry and recreational spaces, and storage for shared resources like tools and lawn mowers. **See www.cohousing.org.**
- **Naturally occurring retirement communities** are arrangements of older adults where residents informally look out for each other. Apartments, condos and mobile home parks are common locations. **See www.thebalance.com /what-is-a-naturally-occurring-retirement -community-4585208.**

Adjusting to a New Community

When you consider moving, decide what you want and need in a new community now and in future life stages.

When you go into a new community, don't wait to be invited to participate in activities. Seek out new opportunities in your neighborhood.

Introduce yourself, mention what you were interested in before and say, "I'd like to be a part of things here."

If you decide to relocate, the success of your move in the long run will be up to you.

Moving Tips

Check if your homeowner's insurance covers your belongings while in transit.

When you move, secure important documents like medical records, power of attorney, birth certificates and Social Security cards, and keep them with you.

If you decide to use a moving company, be mindful. One of the most common kinds of moving fraud is when a mover provides a low-cost quote, loads your belongings onto their truck, claims your load is over the weight estimate and then charges an exorbitant price per pound for the additional weight. The consumer is forced to pay double or higher the original quote just to get their belongings back.

The U.S. Department of Transportation (DOT) can only verify weight estimates, not cubic footage estimates. In general, be wary of movers that charge by the cubic foot, although scammers can overcharge you using either kind of estimate. Here are some tips to avoid moving fraud.

- Get at least three quotes in writing, and have the movers come to your home to evaluate your belongings. Ask about any scenarios in which your moving estimate could increase.
- If possible, get references from people who have actually used the moving company.
- Verify if a mover is a member of the American Moving and Storage Association at **www .moving.org.**
- Ask for DOT and Motor Carrier (MC) identification numbers to see if the movers are registered.

RESEARCHING WHERE TO MOVE

Check out a free online tool called the Livability Index from AARP, where you can see how specific neighborhoods rank in terms of their suitability for aging in place. Go to http://livabilityindex.aarp.org.

Places ranked more livable have:

- Neighborhoods with easy access to stores, restaurants, entertainment, libraries, parks and places to buy healthy food
- Access to quality health care and lower rates of smoking and obesity
- Safe and convenient transportation
- Civic/social engagement in the community
- Internet access
- Diversity, inclusion and economic opportunity
- Clean environment, including healthy air and water.

Check these websites for tips, suggestions on reputable moving companies and consumer complaints:

- **www.movingscam.com**
- **www.fmcsa.dot.gov/protect-your-move.**

If you have experienced fraud, you can file a complaint with the DOT's Federal Motor Carrier Safety Administration (FMCSA) at **www.fmcsa .dot.gov/protect-your-move/file-a-complaint, or call (888) 368-7238.** FMCSA will consider whether to investigate.

Checklist for
Housing

When you are planning where to live in retirement, here are some questions to ask yourself.

Yes No

Where you live now

○ ○   Is my home suitable for retirement living?

○ ○   Can my home be remodeled for satisfactory retirement living?

○ ○   Am I emotionally attached to my home?

○ ○   Is my neighborhood safe?

○ ○   Will I be able to handle the upkeep and maintenance?

○ ○   Will the costs of taxes and insurance be in my budget in retirement?

○ ○   Have I considered using my home equity for income in retirement?

○ ○   Does my home have suitable security or technology?

○ ○   Have I planned how to spend my time?

○ ○   Am I active in my community?

○ ○   Is it important to be near my friends?

○ ○   Is it important to be near my family?

○ ○   Do I want to keep working after I retire?

○ ○   Do I want to stay where I'm known?

○ ○   Do I want to make a fresh start somewhere else?

Before moving to a new area

○ ○   Have I experienced its different seasons?

○ ○   Is it close to shopping and public transportation?

○ ○   Is it near good medical care?

○ ○   Have I gotten legal and financial advice?

○ ○   Have I taken my time with my choices?

Checklist for
Safety

When you are planning how to live independently as long as possible, here are some changes to maximize home safety.

Yes No

○ ○ Do you have no-slip tape in your bathtub or shower?

○ ○ Do you have grab bars and hand grips in showers and bathtubs and near toilets?

○ ○ Can your towel bars and soap holders withstand sudden pulls?

○ ○ Do you keep throw rugs away from the tops and bottoms of stairs?

○ ○ Do all rugs have no-slip mats under them?

○ ○ Do you have wheelchair access such as ramps, wider doorways and a roll-in shower?

○ ○ Are all chairs and stairs sturdy and free of wobbles?

○ ○ Have you replaced all frayed cords and broken plugs?

○ ○ Have you relocated all furniture, lamp cords and clutter from traffic paths?

○ ○ Do you avoid running extension cords under rugs or carpets?

○ ○ Do you avoid using space heaters, if possible? If they are necessary, are they away from flammable materials and out of traffic lanes?

○ ○ Do you make sure you do not smoke while lying down?

○ ○ Have you installed smoke, heat and carbon monoxide detectors throughout the house?

○ ○ Have you installed fire extinguishers near the kitchen and workroom?

○ ○ Do you have escape routes planned from all areas of the home in case of fire?

○ ○ Do you avoid overloading one socket with several plugs?

○ ○ Have you discarded heavy, hard-to-handle or broken cooking utensils?

○ ○ Are there handrails on all stairs and inclines?

○ ○ Have you installed night-lights in the bedroom, bathroom and hallways?

○ ○ Have you made sure stairways and other areas are well-lit?

○ ○ Do you have a flashlight by the bed?

○ ○ If you live alone, do you have a neighbor, friend or relative check in with you at regular intervals?

○ ○ Do you keep a first-aid kit and emergency phone numbers handy? Have you taken a first-aid course or CPR course?

Earning Money

"An investment in knowledge pays the best interest."

—Benjamin Franklin

Working in Retirement

Do you have to work after retirement? Many people who could answer "no" to this question from a purely economic point of view would still say "yes" from a psychological one.

For many, of course, this question is decided in terms of economic necessity. Work is essential for adequate income.

But there are reasons to work beyond having enough income to live comfortably. Some people work because it is satisfying and personally fulfilling. Some consider work to be part of their identity. Some find retirement boring or lacking social connection.

Americans are living longer and healthier lives, and many retirees prefer a combination of work and leisure to fill their needs. In fact, given a choice, most older workers would prefer continuing with some kind of employment. Work contributes to our lives in a way that is not easily replaced by anything else.

WHY WORK IN RETIREMENT?

To keep mentally active	**62**%
To keep physically active	**46**%
To keep connected with others	**42**%
A sense of self-worth	**36**%
To make money	**31**%
New challenges	**30**%
Health insurance	**11**%

Source: Merrill Lynch and Age Wave survey of age 50+ working retirees.

Satisfactions That Come With a Job

- It is a basis for self-respect and the feeling that you have something to contribute.

- It is a source of prestige and recognition. People appreciate your ability to perform.
- It provides a place for social participation.
- Many friendships are related to the job.

- It is a source of enjoyment and a chance to be creative.
- It is a way of helping others.
- It helps give order to the day and makes time pass. You don't have to plan for or organize a great part of the day.
- It helps provide finances to pay the bills, enjoy a dinner out or take a vacation.

Start Planning Early

If you're five to ten years away from retirement, or even midcareer, it's not too early to plan for retirement career interests. If you'd like to switch careers, this is the time to learn new skills through training or education. Also consider that job markets fluctuate and layoffs or mergers can happen, meaning people may find themselves looking for a new job or career, not by choice, at a relatively early age. Engaging in ongoing training and learning can allow you to hit the ground running. Early planning while you're still working is beneficial if you hope to be an entrepreneur in retirement. **(See page 123.)**

Get all the training opportunities you can from your current employer. A lot of community college, university and graduate programs are offered on evenings, weekends or online. Check if your employer has a tuition reimbursement program, reimbursement for earning a professional designation or a discounted college benefit. Be sure to ask about any program rules. Some employers make you repay tuition if you leave within a few years after completing the education. If your employer offers paid days off to volunteer, that's another opportunity to gain experience and make professional connections.

Unintended Consequences

- If you plan to work and receive Social Security, be aware that there is a yearly limit on the amount of earnings you can make before withholding some of your benefits. **(See Chapter 3.)**

- If you are covered by Medicare, you should consider whether a new employer's insurance benefits will change your coverage. The rules depend on employer size. **(See Chapter 8.)**
- Earning income from a job could bump you into a higher income tax bracket. That could affect the taxes you pay on 401(k) or similar tax-deferred retirement savings plans.
- Your spending may go up in the budget categories of clothing, dining out and transportation. Compare these costs with your potential income to make sure you feel comfortable with the math. Or perhaps limit your job search to work-at-home opportunities if that proves to be better for your budget.

Believe in Yourself

If you've been fully retired for a while, it's natural to ask yourself questions like: If I wish to work, will I be able to find a job? Who will be interested in having an individual who has been retired from active work? How can I compete with younger workers in terms of strength, ability to learn and contribution to the company?

The greatest obstacle to finding employment may be the attitude that you have about yourself. It's true that there are a number of misconceptions about older workers, but there also are some noted strengths. Focus on the positive things that you have to offer.

Myths About Older Workers

The Department of Labor and other agencies have studied the performance of older workers and have come up with the following facts that refute the myths about them.

Myth: Older workers are too slow. They can't meet production requirements.

Fact: There is no significant drop in performance and productivity. In fact, many older workers exceed the average output of younger employees.

Chapter 10 **Earning Money**

Myth: Older workers can't meet the physical demands of jobs.

Fact: Few jobs require great strength or heavy lifting. Labor-saving equipment makes it possible to handle jobs without difficulty.

Myth: Older workers are absent too often.

Fact: The attendance of workers over 65 compares favorably with other age groups.

Myth: Older workers are inflexible. They're hard to train because they can't accept change.

Fact: Adaptability depends on the individual, not on age. Some young people are set in their ways, while a high proportion of older workers show flexibility in accepting a change in occupation and earnings.

Myth: Hiring older workers increases our pension and insurance costs.

Fact: Most pension plans provide for benefits related to length of service, earnings or both. Small, additional pensions, when incurred, can be more than offset by work experience, lower turnover and quality of work. The costs of group life, accident and health insurance and workers' compensation are not materially increased by hiring older workers.

Attitudes Toward Older Workers

Which favorable or unfavorable attitudes toward older workers apply to you?

Favorable
- Sound judgment
- Wastes less time on job than younger workers
- Less absenteeism; more apt to stay on the job
- Safe work habits
- Greater sense of responsibility
- Good appearance
- Once trained, requires less supervision
- Stability that comes with maturity. Less distracted by outside interests, has fewer domestic troubles and is capable of greater concentration

Unfavorable
- Defeatist attitude toward getting work and difficult time impressing an employer
- Feeling like you are slowing down and sharing this with a prospective employer
- Forgotten how to go about getting a job
- Reluctant to change occupations even if there is no work available in line with previous work
- Refuses to consider jobs paying less or having less prestige because of personal pride
- Doesn't know limitations and makes unrealistic demands for wages, location, working conditions, etc.
- Tends to undersell self and fails to impress prospective employers

What Do You Want to Do?

Some people choose to switch to a second career after retirement for the opportunity to feel productive and do something they are passionate about. You may be in your second career for the next ten or 20 years. Match your interests, skills, experiences and current situation while looking for a job. You need to look at all of these factors to get a total picture. You may be interested in doing something for which you have little experience. You may not like the kind of work in which you have experience. Try brainstorming some answers to the following questions.

Past Jobs Held
- What did you like and dislike?
- What made you feel rewarded?
- What motivated you?

Skills and Abilities
- What can you do best?
- What talents do you have?
- Where are your skills needed?

Educational Qualifications
- Have you had special instruction?

Physical Limitations

- Does your health rule out some jobs?

Interests and Passions

- What did you dream of doing as a child or young adult?
- What would you do if money was no object?

Goals

- What would be ideal for you?
- What have you always wanted to do?
- What do you enjoy doing?

Your Resumé

The goal of your resumé is to get an interview. Customize it for each job you apply for. Be sure your resumé is clear and understandable. Highlight your experience relevant to the job. Start with your accomplishments, focus on ways you excelled and show how your skills can contribute to the company. Use keywords; many companies digitize resumés by searching for keywords. Be honest, and avoid lies or exaggerations.

Employers cannot legally ask how old you are but, from your resumé, they can guess. Leave graduation dates off your resumé. Be careful with other dates you include. For early positions, don't add irrelevant jobs. List a category called Prior Positions Held and leave out dates. If using email, send the resumé in the body of the email since it could get caught in a spam folder or the employer may be unable to open an attachment. Some companies will require you to include your salary requirements when you apply for the job or submit your resumé. Be realistic.

For more information, visit CareerOneStop's Resume Guide at www.careeronestop.org /JobSearch/Resumes/resumes.aspx.

The Job Interview

Your goal for an interview is to get a job offer. Prepare for the interview ahead of time by practicing with a friend and/or speaking out loud, even if you're by yourself in front of a mirror.

- A typical first question is: "Tell me a little about yourself." Practice how you will answer, and customize your response to the job. Highlight a relevant, recent accomplishment and some past experiences that made it possible to get where you are today, and then end with why you're interested in the job.
- Interviewers are using more and more behavioral questions that require you to share how you have performed and dealt with issues in the past as a way to determine your capabilities if you're hired. Practice telling brief stories about how you solved a problem or led a team project. **(See box on page 122.)**
- Research the industry and the specific organization so you can tailor your answers to their business needs.

The key is to define yourself in a way that fits the position. Focus on how you can add value to the organization. You will likely be talking to someone younger than yourself. Avoid saying things like "When I was your age . . ." to show the interviewer that you are open-minded and forward-looking.

The interview is not the time to talk about pay expectations or your desire for a flexible schedule. Save that for when you get a job offer. The job may pay less than what you earned before retirement. Discuss your skills and experience realistically. Negotiating for higher wages or more perks is possible, depending on the industry and job level in an organization.

To leave a favorable impression at your interview:

- Be poised and confident but not cocky
- Be pleasant but businesslike
- Speak firmly and clearly
- Listen attentively to your interviewer's questions
- Answer briefly and honestly
- Stress your stability and good attendance record
- Ask intelligent questions about the job
- Research the company, and read the company's website
- Bring copies of your resumé, and tailor it to the job description

Your Experience Inventory

Employment Objective (As clearly and concisely as possible, indicate what you want to do.)

_____

_____

Employment History (List employment in reverse chronological order.)

Job Title and Responsibilities   Company Name and Location

_____

_____

_____

Miscellaneous Employment (List part-time and/or minor employment, if these would help.)

_____

_____

_____

Education (List schools in reverse chronological order.)

Name of School and Location   Degree/Last Grade Completed

_____

_____

_____

Additional Education (List online courses, company courses, seminars, certifications, professional designations, etc.)

_____

_____

Professional Associations (List organizations to which you belong or did belong.)

_____

_____

Interests (List volunteer activities and hobbies, especially if they relate to the job you want.)

_____

_____

_____

STAR INTERVIEW TECHNIQUE

Behavioral interview questions often start with:

- Tell me about a time when . . .
- Have you ever . . .
- Give me an example of . . .
- Describe a . . .

Your goal in responding to these questions is to share a fitting example with some detail in an understandable way without rambling. That sounds like a lot to fit in.

The STAR acronym helps people tell a meaningful story about a past work experience.

- Situation: Set the scene and give the necessary details of your example.
- Task: Describe what your responsibility was in that situation.
- Action: Explain exactly what steps you took to address it.
- Result: Share what outcomes your actions achieved.

For more details and examples, go to www.themuse.com/advice/star-interview -method.

- Show the interviewer that you are interested in the job
- Describe how you solved a problem if you are asked about difficult moments
- Stress your skills and tell brief, specific stories about them, i.e., problem solving, interpersonal communications, reading comprehension, customer skills and basic computer skills
- Leave when the interview is over, thanking the employer for the opportunity

- Write a handwritten thank-you note after the interview.

Do not get dejected if you do not receive the job; many may have applied. Thank the interviewer, and ask them to keep you in mind for future job opportunities.

How Not to Impress

Poor impressions are left by those who:
- Are timid and ill at ease
- Are stubborn and argumentative
- Stress their need for a job
- Emphasize their age, limitations or personal problems
- Exaggerate their skills
- Criticize a former employer
- Talk too long
- Show reluctance to give references or take necessary exams.

Job Search Sources

There are sources of help for locating a job or developing the skills needed to get one, including:
- Friends, relatives, former co-workers or other members of your social circle. Tell them that you're looking for a job, and ask them for help in finding one.
- College placement offices
- Public libraries
- Company websites
- Industrial and craft unions
- Private employment agencies (some charge a fee) or nonprofit employment agencies
- Professional associations
- Temporary agencies. Temporary jobs can lead to permanent positions.
- 40Plus organizations for executives in major cities
- Online job sites
  General
  - **www.LinkedIn.com**
  - **www.careeronestop.org**

- **www.careerbuilder.com**
- **www.monster.com**
- **www.glassdoor.com**
- **www.indeed.com**

Specialized

- **www.workforce50.com**
- **www.retirementjobs.com**
- **www.themuse.com** (job-seeking advice and career coaching)
- **www.military.com/veteran-jobs** (military-friendly companies)
- **www.moaa.org** (Military Officers Association of America; for members)
- **www.retiredbrains.com**
- **www.coolworks.com** (focuses on outdoor and adventurous workplaces)
- **www.encore.org** (focuses on opportunities for people age 50 and over. The *encore career* is one that often pays less but provides meaning, the potential for new skills and a chance to help people. Jobs in education, social services and public services are typical.)

- ■ Your state Department of Labor
- ■ National Council on Aging. The Senior Community Service Employment Program helps people age 55 and over return to or remain active in the workforce by providing job training, job search services and on-the-job experience. **Go to www.ncoa.org/economic -security/matureworkers/scsep.**

Identity Theft Risk

Be careful about putting your resumé online; it could lead to identity theft. Use job sites that allow you to hide your contact information and where an employer must click on a link to email you. If you must make your information public, use your first initial, omit your street address and phone number, and set up a temporary email address. Do not give out your Social Security number until you verify that the recruiter and position are for real.

Working for Yourself

If you want to have a good job interview with a person you really like and have your resumé read by admiring and sympathetic eyes, try making an application to yourself for a job! It's safe to say that you can work out hours that are agreeable to employer and employee. For these reasons and many more, some retirees will want to consider being their own boss.

One option is to be self-employed in the gig economy. The other is to own your own business. The highest rate of entrepreneurship is between the ages of 55 and 64, and 25% of workers 65 and older are self-employed. Those who use their life experiences have a greater chance of success.

There are many ways this can be done.

Gig Economy

In the *gig economy*—also known as the *sharing* or *on demand* economy—websites or apps connect independent workers with customers for a specific service. A growing number of older adults are earning money this way. Thirty percent of Americans over the age of 55 did some *freelance work,* meaning any work that is independently contracted, according to a study by the Freelancers Union and Upwork. That number is expected to increase as more Baby Boomers reach retirement age.

More than 10,000 websites and smartphone apps offer gig work. Many skills and hobbies can be monetized. Some common gig work is driving for a ride-sharing service, renting out part of your home on a short-term basis, babysitting, pet sitting, and restaurant and grocery delivery. There are pros and cons. You have the freedom to set your schedule and choose what you want to do, along with lots of social interaction. But being self-employed also means that you're responsible for income tax payment, your income can vary and you won't be offered employee benefits. It is also important to research gig economy employers to make sure they are legitimate enterprises. Be wary of any business that asks you to invest your own money before you get paid. (See "Job and Business Opportunity Scams" on page 73 for more information.)

The best way to see if freelance work is right for you is to talk to the people who are already doing it.

Choosing Your Business

Operating a part-time business may be an opportunity to supplement your income and find meaningful ways to invest your time. If it is done on a small scale, it may not require too much capital and know-how.

Considerable caution should be exercised, however, in the selection of a business. On average, your chances of remaining in your business for three years are about 50/50. A Dun and Bradstreet survey revealed that 90% of such business failures were due to inexperience. Considering the high failure rate in business and the possibility of overextending yourself in demands on your money, health and time, get plenty of information, and be sure that you know what you need before going into business. Be realistic.

Another factor is the current business climate of chain stores, online stores and big corporations. Ideally, your choice of business would not lead you to compete against these types of entities and their vast resources.

Try to get an early start on preparing for the business you will operate in retirement. You will need time to familiarize yourself with the business, accumulate investment capital and purchase necessary equipment before attempting to live on a retirement budget.

You must do research. Find out who needs your product or service and who you will compete against.

Answering the questions listed below should give you some insights into the type of business that best suits you.
- How well do I get along with other people?
- Am I ready to assume responsibility for payroll and business obligations?
- Am I a good organizer?

- Do I like the proposed business enough to sacrifice for it?
- Am I prepared to take the risk involved in owning a business?
- Do I like to sell?
- Can I make decisions and live with them?
- How do I react to emergencies?
- Do I want to start from scratch or buy a franchise?
- Do I know a small business owner who may be interested in bringing on a business partner?

For help on starting and running a small business:
- **U.S. Small Business Administration (SBA) www.sba.gov**
- **SCORE, an organization that can help entrepreneurs through mentoring, workshops and educational resources. www.score.org**

Your Business Plan

If you wish to start your own business, preparing a good business plan is the first step. If you need financing or want to bring your bank manager on board in case you run into problems, you'll need a business plan. Having a thorough one demonstrates that you are a self-starter who has put a great deal of thought into your business idea.

Aside from money matters, a business plan will help the overall management of your new enterprise. Getting the business plan right can mean the difference between success and failure.

What does a good business plan look like? Each business plan is different but, in general, it should include:
- A description of the business, including short- and long-term goals
- Analysis of the market being entered (including a discussion of competitors' strengths and weaknesses and your competitive advantage)
- Financial details including start-up costs, the size of the investment required, and profit and cash-flow projections for a minimum of one year ahead.

Running a Business Out of Your Home

Having your business where you live eliminates some of the costs of operating from a separate location. You do not have to worry about paying rent for the business, nor do you have to incur transportation costs getting to and from work.

It will also be easier to maintain a schedule that is more relaxed if you are working out of your own home.

One warning, though: Check for any zoning regulations or licensing procedures that might be required to run a business in a private home. Also, be sure you're covered by adequate insurance.

Franchises

This is the kind of business venture that has some of the features of owning your own business and some of the features of working for somebody else. You have to put up some capital, but often the national organization has standards and methods of operation that are part of your obligation to the jointly owned business. The organization often will assume responsibility for giving you training and will supervise the market so that no unfair competition will arise from another member of the same organization.

Franchises are really a form of licensing. The franchisor, which is usually an owner of a service, product or method, distributes through affiliated dealers who are the franchises. If you purchase a franchise, often you will be given exclusive rights to the area served by your franchise. But you can still run into trouble from other companies offering similar franchises, so be careful to check beforehand for competition in your area.

A franchise should be carefully investigated before the decision is made to invest in it.

Many fraudulent promoters are at work in the field, offering schemes that are little more than obligations on the part of the victims to purchase supplies or goods from the promoters.

CHARACTERISTICS OF ENTREPRENEURS

The U.S. Small Business Administration lists ten characteristics that businesspeople should have.

Rank yourself by 1 (exceptional), 2 (above average), 3 (average), 4 (below average) or 5 (deficient) to find your business potential.

Trait	Rank
Initiative	_____
Positive attitude	_____
Leadership ability	_____
Organizing ability	_____
Industry	_____
Responsibility	_____
Quick and accurate judgments	_____
Sincerity	_____
Perseverance	_____
High level of energy	_____

The more "1s" and "2s" you have listed, the easier it will be for you to adjust to running a business.

Good advice is available from Better Business Bureaus, Chambers of Commerce and others, so be sure to have adequate information before venturing into this business.

Working for Others

There are jobs that are directly related to service for others, and the compensation is a combination of a modest paycheck and the knowledge that you have made life more rewarding for someone else. These jobs take as much of your time as you care to give. Volunteering also is a way to share your time with others, and it can lead to employment opportunities because some employers pick employees from their volunteer groups. **(See Chapter 12.)**

Be Prepared

If you are seriously interested in developing the skills necessary to go back to work or start your own business, two of the best places to go for information and help are your public library and your local college.

Libraries have resources on job searches and entrepreneurship.

Colleges, particularly community colleges, also provide services for job seekers. In addition to courses that can develop skills and expertise in specific areas (such as business, accounting or education), many colleges offer classes—including online courses—designed for adults who wish to know more about developing second careers and getting back into the employment mainstream.

Leisure

"Aging is an extraordinary process where you become the person you always should have been."

—David Bowie

Leisure Time

In your working years and/or child-rearing years, time spent on leisure is infrequent and limited to short periods of time. But, in retirement, planning how you will spend your time is just as important as planning how you will spend your money.

Plan for your everyday leisure as well as bucket list ideas or major leisure goals you hope to achieve. This chapter will provide you with an opportunity to look at yourself and to consider the alternatives available for structuring your time. You'll explore what adjustments may be necessary to meet your basic needs as you attempt to fill your life with meaning that is not derived specifically from work.

Retirement should be a transition from toil to leisure. It should see a transfer of the energies you formerly devoted to making a living to the new business of living well. In the transition, you will learn to reallocate your time. Avoid making a financial commitment to any leisure activity until you are sure that your interest won't disappear as you devote more time to it. Keep your budget and any health-related challenges in mind when thinking about realistic leisure plans.

Choosing How to Spend Your Time

Answering these questions will lead you into an examination of yourself: who you really are, what you really want, what your attitude is toward the use of your time, etc.

- Will your leisure be aimless or a time when you discover how to enjoy life as never before?
- Will your use of leisure time result in success or failure in your attempt to achieve happiness during retirement?
- How much leisure time will you have on your hands? What will your schedule be like after full-time employment is no longer the major part of your daytime activities?
- What will replace the satisfaction that work has afforded?
- When you were a child, what did you love most?
- Who matters to you?
- What makes you feel relaxed?
- Are you motivated by goal-setting for any nonwork activities?
- How do you describe your ideal day? Would you want to do this every day?

- Do you want to do familiar activities, new activities or a combination of the two?
- Does planning ahead increase or decrease your anxiety?

Vacation: Each Day of the Year

A vacation is a vacation because it comes infrequently, but a vacation every day of the year? That's something else entirely.

Your happiness in retirement may be strongly linked to the activities you pursue. Planning will help you to enjoy a diverse range of meaningful and satisfying activities instead of just mindlessly filling up time. Unplanned time can lead to boredom, feelings of guilt and a sense of frustration. Most people do not stumble upon an activity they love just because they've retired. Remember to build quality into your leisure hours.

What you love to do may change throughout your retirement years. Change is a constant in life. Don't have a plan that is overly precise because you need to remain open to the possibilities and hardships that life will bring.

Can Work Be More Fun?

Many people prefer to work even when it is not an economic necessity. A study at the Duke University Center for Aging revealed that more than half of the 400 people surveyed said they got more satisfaction from work than they did from leisure. This preference for work over free time held true for women (55%) and men (52%).

Can You Accept Leisure?

You need to decide if you can accept the free time you have earned. To really enjoy leisure, you will have to learn to not work. Teach yourself that it is right for you to enjoy doing something for the pleasure it brings. Retrain your mind to accept that leisure is not inactivity and that nonwork activities

may be as necessary and useful as those for which we formerly received paychecks.

It's a good idea to try to replace work colleagues with other networks, rediscover play, uncover new passions and continue learning.

The goal in retirement is not just to fill your time but to fill it in a meaningful way. Fulfilling leisure time has the following characteristics.

- We do it because we want to.
- We anticipate it and remember it fondly.
- We may do it alone or with others.
- We feel good about it.
- It contributes to others as well as to ourselves.
- We may do it for fun or profit.

Leisure can affect your health and your wealth. We can lose both if our bodies and minds are wasted through inactivity or in useless occupation.

Learn to enjoy leisure. Work if you wish, and be as active in your retirement as you care to be, but accept the fact that it's OK to enjoy many different activities, including the activity of doing nothing.

Adding Spice to Your Life

What you do with your everyday leisure time should be more than being busy. Those activities that are worth your time should:

- Create excitement
- Stimulate you and give you renewed zest
- Be both physically and intellectually stimulating.

If in a relationship, have your partner consider the same categories—then compare, and see what things you have in common to explore together in retirement.

Maintaining or improving your health can be an ideal, everyday leisure pursuit. Social connections are important for everyday leisure too, whether they be with a spouse or partner, friends, grandkids, neighbors or others in your community.

Also worth your time is writing down those bucket list ideas—rare, unique or special activities you want to experience—and perhaps special people you want to share experiences with.

Need for Leisure Activities

There are some basic needs that remain constant throughout life, and many of these can be met through a wise selection of leisure activities. Look at some of these basic needs, and see how they compare with your present leisure activities. Alongside the corresponding need, list an activity you are presently engaged in that makes a contribution to that need. In the right-hand column, list additional activities that you would like to consider in the future to meet that need.

Need	Present Activities	Projected Activities
Recognition		
Entertainment		
Self-expression, creativity		
Participation, belonging		
Adventure, new experience		
Learning		
Security		
Physical fitness		
Contemplation		
Self-growth		
Feeling useful		
Income		

What's Best for You?

Enjoying an activity is one good reason for considering it, but there are other factors to consider. Activities that often bring satisfaction to people include the following qualities.

- Basic skills can be mastered readily
- Real proficiency can come with practice
- So many facets that it doesn't become tiresome
- Within your budget
- Enlarges a skill you already possess
- Offers opportunity for self-development
- Provides a change of pace from your routine
- Can be practiced all year long
- Represents a blend of several activities
- Can be pursued in spite of some physical limitations

- Puts you in touch with other people
- Provides challenges to improve, grow or become more proficient in an area of interest

Travel Information

Many people wish to travel for fun in retirement.

Bed and breakfast

The Evergreen Club provides B&B hospitality for those over age 50 in private homes for a modest gratuity. **www.evergreenclub.com**

Outdoor

You can buy an *America the Beautiful* Senior Pass for $80 at age 62 and, for the rest of your life, you will be admitted free to all national parks, monuments and recreation areas and receive half off federal user fees for certain facilities and services. **www.nps.gov/planyourvisit/passes.htm**

Educational group travel

- Road Scholar—**www.roadscholar.org**
- Smithsonian Journeys— **www.smithsonianjourneys.org**

Get off the road and check out a train or boating vacation.

- **www.VacationsByRail.com**
- **www.houseboating.org**

Bike tours

- Senior Cycling provides comfortable, safe, small-group bike tours. **www.seniorcycling.com**

Active

- Overseas Adventure Travel (O.A.T.) travelers are typically over age 50. **www.oattravel.com**
- Mountain Travel Sobek—**www.mtsobek.com**
- REI Adventures—**www.rei.com/adventures**
- National Geographic— **www.nationalgeographic.com/expeditions**

Travel Tips

- Single travelers can find tips about destinations, safety and saving money at **www .solotravelerworld.com.**
- Consider buying travel insurance.
- Medicare usually does not cover health care while you are traveling outside the United States. Medigap policies may offer coverage.
- While traveling by car, take hourly walks, if possible, to help with circulation. If you're on a plane, get up and move around every hour, if possible. While you're seated, stretch your legs and flex your feet. Do not cross your legs at the ankles or knees. This will help blood move toward the heart.
- Drink plenty of fluids—and avoid caffeine or alcohol—to stay hydrated.
- Before traveling overseas, check with your doctor.
- Call your credit card issuer to notify them of your travel plans and find out about foreign conversion fees.
- Check with your mobile phone carrier for an international phone plan to avoid high roaming charges.

Travel Safety

- Before traveling, make copies of key documents. Take one copy with you, and leave another set at home with a family member or friend.
- Do not publicize your travel on social-networking sites.
- For travel warnings and other information, check the U.S. State Department at **www .travel.state.gov.**
- Check the Centers for Disease Control at **www .cdc. gov/travel.**
- Give the U.S. government your itinerary at Free Smart Traveler's Enrollment Program (STEP) at **https://step.state.gov** so someone can contact you and assist you in an emergency.

Checklist for
Possible Leisure Activities

Active
- ○ Barre
- ○ Bicycling
- ○ Bowling
- ○ CrossFit
- ○ Dancing
- ○ Golf
- ○ Hiking
- ○ Jogging
- ○ Kayaking
- ○ Martial arts
- ○ Rock climbing
- ○ Surfing
- ○ Swimming
- ○ Tai Chi
- ○ Tennis
- ○ Walking
- ○ Yoga
- ○ Zumba

Mental
- ○ Chess
- ○ Games
- ○ Meditation
- ○ Puzzles
- ○ Reading
- ○ Spiritual activities
- ○ Time to be alone

Social
- ○ Book club
- ○ Card-playing club
- ○ Charitable activities
- ○ Coaching
- ○ Community projects
- ○ Dice club
- ○ Entertaining
- ○ Family activities
- ○ Festivals
- ○ Historical societies
- ○ Politics
- ○ Sporting events

Outdoors
- ○ Bird watching
- ○ Boating
- ○ Camping
- ○ Enjoying nature
- ○ Fishing
- ○ Gardening

Educational
- ○ Art galleries
- ○ Astronomy
- ○ DIY projects/repairs
- ○ Documentaries
- ○ Genealogy
- ○ Movies
- ○ Museums
- ○ New language
- ○ Teaching/tutoring
- ○ Traveling
- ○ TV/subscription services

Creative
- ○ 3-D printing
- ○ Acting
- ○ Antiquing
- ○ Baking
- ○ Beer brewing
- ○ Blogging
- ○ Collecting
- ○ Cooking
- ○ Crafts
- ○ Jewelry making
- ○ Knitting/crochet
- ○ Lego
- ○ Origami
- ○ Painting
- ○ Photography
- ○ Pottery
- ○ Scrapbooking
- ○ Sewing/quilting
- ○ Woodworking
- ○ Writing

Musical
- ○ Choir
- ○ Composing music
- ○ Concerts
- ○ Handbells
- ○ Practicing musical instrument(s)

Volunteer

"We make a living by what we get, but we make a life by what we give."

—Winston Churchill

Meaningful Use of Time

In the preceding chapters, you looked at the amount of time you are going to have during retirement and some suggestions for making the most of it through leisure and earning money. You took a good look at yourself and how to fill your time with experiences that give you pleasure.

In this chapter, you can do the same thing but in a different light. After all, you probably won't be able to find continual happiness thinking only about yourself. Because of the sheer fun of sharing, many people feel great satisfaction in giving a part of themselves to community service activities.

The philosopher Albert Schweitzer notes that wherever people turn, they can find someone who needs them. "Even if it is a little thing, do something for which you get no pay but the privilege of doing it. For remember, you don't live in a world all your own." Volunteer work does not have to be for long periods of time, but it does involve the sharing of personal time and interests and participation with others toward a common objective.

When to Begin

You do not have to wait for retirement to begin volunteer work. You can start on a limited basis, as time permits, and extend your service in retirement. This will give you a chance to practice. Some companies encourage employees approaching retirement to devote time before retirement to community service. This permits a gradual transfer of interests and skills to a service-oriented job as formal employment draws to a close. Volunteering as a way to make new friends and try new activities can be especially important if you have not maintained outside interests during your working years. By starting volunteer work now, you will be going into retirement with an established circle of friends whose interests are similar to your own.

Volunteering Benefits You and Your Community

Research has shown that volunteering can improve your quality of life; the benefits include higher self-esteem and a greater sense of well-being. Numerous studies have shown that giving and volunteering are associated with lower rates of depression, blood pressure and mortality. Volunteering also is a way to feel productive and stay active.

Volunteering broadens your social connections. Being involved with people helps keep the mind sharp, and relationships can reduce stress and limit the effects of aging.

Another plus for volunteer service: It is good work experience. If you are thinking about starting a second career, volunteer work can provide the background needed to reach your goal. Or if you are considering a certain line of work but have some doubts, volunteer service may be just the way to help you know for sure.

Service Instead of Salary

You may not have realized the degree to which your sense of personal worth has been related to your job. During your early and middle working years, you have a definite (at times almost overwhelming) sense of responsibility. You contribute to society through your work. You may be needed by your family or friends.

Community service activities in retirement offer you such job-related satisfactions as:
- Camaraderie with other people
- A chance for recognition
- An opportunity to contribute to a useful goal
- An opportunity to belong to a worthy group.

The extent of participation is up to the volunteer. It can be as little as an hour a week. It can be much more. It can be a minimum of personal involvement, with only routine chores, or it can be deeply personal.

Choosing the Best Activity

There are so many needs that you have the luxury of choosing one or more to match your interests and skills.

Ask yourself the following questions when considering how to invest your time.

VOLUNTEER OPPORTUNITIES

On the following list, check the skills that you do well and would like to share.

- ○ Bookkeeping
- ○ Caregiving
- ○ Carpentry
- ○ Computers
- ○ Cooking
- ○ Entertaining
- ○ Gardening
- ○ Hunting
- ○ Leadership
- ○ Legal experience
- ○ Medical experience
- ○ Music
- ○ Organizing
- ○ Photography
- ○ Sales
- ○ Speaking
- ○ Teaching
- ○ Visiting
- ○ Writing

- Is it something about which I care deeply?
- Does it require a skill I possess?
- Does it provide association with enjoyable people?
- Does it require time I am prepared to give?
- Do I enjoy doing it?

Where to Volunteer

There are groups in every community involved in a variety of interests. Many are intergenerational, creating a diverse and interesting atmosphere. Check these local places of interest to you.
- Animal shelters
- Centers for people of all abilities
- Child care centers
- Community colleges
- Donation centers
- Elder care centers

- Food banks
- Gardens
- Homeless shelters
- Hospitals
- Libraries
- Literacy programs
- Museums
- Parks
- Recreation departments
- Schools
- Senior centers
- Social, civic, political, nonprofit and spiritual groups represented in your community

On these websites, you can find volunteer opportunities ranging from local to global.

- National Park Service— www.NPS.gov/getinvolved/volunteer.htm
- NECS National Executive Service Corps— www.nesc.org
- The Peace Corps—www.peacecorps.gov
- The Points of Light—www.pointsoflight.org
- Senior Corps—www.nationalservice.gov /programs/senior-corps (foster grandparenting and senior companions)
- Volunteer Match— www.volunteermatch.org

Keep Up to Date

"I am not young enough to know everything."

—Oscar Wilde

For an Exciting Retirement

Continuing your education is another consideration when it comes to planning how to spend your time in retirement. Perhaps it's time to think about going back to school. This chapter will provide ideas of what you could study and how. There are many options in addition to college that will allow you to explore the possibilities of enriching your life through learning.

Maintain Mental Sharpness

If you have a lively mind and an interest in improving it, you almost certainly can find educational opportunities (often free or at minimal charge) that can open up a world of vast horizons in your later years.

The sharpness of a mind is generally blunted not by age but by disuse. This can happen at any age.

Those who are reasonably healthy can maintain the ability to learn new things well into their later years. If mental responses are slowed a little, this is more than offset by the fact that the older you are, the greater your advantage in being able to apply your background of knowledge and experience.

So don't hold back or feel awkward about going back to school or being taught by a younger person.

High School Equivalency

Many people are interested in making up for years when going to school was not possible.

There are four legitimate high school equivalency tests: GED, HiSET, TASC and, for California only, the CHSPE. Each state approves at least one test. The approved tests vary by state, and some states approve more than one.

Another way to get your diploma in some states is to take classes and earn credits. Classes that meet the requirements might be offered by community colleges, college extension programs, and adult education programs run by local high schools, school boards, nonprofits, state departments of education or state workforce programs.

If a program says you can earn your diploma with just life experience, it's almost certainly a scam.

The best way to find a legitimate program is to contact your state's department of education. To find out more about high school diploma scams, go to www.consumer.ftc.gov/articles/0539-high -school-diploma-scams.

Colleges or Universities

- Undergraduate or graduate degrees
- Extension programs
- Lifelong Learning Institutes (LLI). To find one, go to www.osherfoundation.org or lli.roadscholar.org/find-an-lli-near-you.
- Institutes for Learning in Retirement (ILR)

Community-Based Programs

- Community or technical colleges
- Public schools
- Libraries
- Museums
- Galleries
- Recreation departments
- Ecology centers
- Senior centers

More Ways to Learn

- Book clubs (fiction or nonfiction)
- Books or audiobooks
- Online courses
  - www.coursera.org
  - www.khanacademy.org
- Podcasts
- Television and video subscription services
- Webcasts

If You Are Interested in College

If you are among those who didn't go to college or complete college work toward a degree, now might be a time to get started. Or if you are among those with keen interests in a field that differs from your main occupation, it can be a good time to satisfy them by looking through a college catalog and signing up for a course or two. The range of classes is likely wider than other types of adult education programs, and the subject matter is probably more advanced.

To find out what is available and what the entrance requirements will be—and which coursework counts toward a degree, if that is your goal—you should contact the admissions department.

Weekend classes may be an option if you prefer that schedule to attending class several times per week.

If you take courses for credit, you will have to meet the same requirements and be graded the same way as all other students: attending classes, doing assigned work, turning in papers and taking exams.

Tuition and Debt

Tuition costs are high and continually rising. Ask about tuition discounts for older students or scholarships for nontraditional students. Some colleges may allow you to audit a class (receiving no credit) for a nominal fee or for free. Review your budget to ensure you have the cash flow to pay for tuition right away.

Watch out for student loan debt. If you are thinking about taking out a student loan, consider whether it is possible to set a short-term savings goal for tuition and delay school until you have met it. According to AARP, default rates on student loan debt have become a threat to Americans' retirement

COURSES OF ALL KINDS

Academic

- Art or music appreciation
- Business
- Classic books and literature
- Communications
- Current events
- Geography
- History
- Languages
- Philosophy
- Physical sciences
- Political science
- Sociology
- Technology
- Writing

Practical

Courses can be invaluable during your retirement years, when money is tight. The skills you learn not only can provide personal satisfaction but also can save you money, which can help in your fight against inflation.

- Budgeting and investing
- Cooking
- Health
- Home and auto repairs
- Legal and tax matters
- Sewing

Other classes are oriented toward hobbies and offer chances to explore ways to spend your retirement leisure time. See Chapter 11 for ideas.

Job Training

- Bookkeeping
- Computer programming
- Medical technology
- Office skills
- Real estate
- Starting your own business

security. The federal government may take up to 15% out of defaulted borrowers' monthly Social Security benefits.

For any of the education options mentioned in this chapter, you can always ask if there is a senior discount.

Advantages of Learning

Education can lead to a happier and more interesting retirement. With a little time, energy and motivation, you can use these opportunities for continuing education to help yourself feel younger, more alive and more stimulated.

Families, Couples and Singles

"People will forget what you said, people will forget what you did, but people will never forget how you made them feel."

—Maya Angelou

Planning With People Who Support You

Ideally, both married and single people should begin retirement planning by their mid-50s or earlier. But do not be discouraged if you are well past that age. Regardless of your age, it is a good idea to assess your assets and liabilities as soon as possible. Summarize your entire financial position, whether you are single, married and/or with kids. By now you've bought insurance, made your will and maybe discussed retirement with your spouse, friends and/or family. Have you, however, been realistic and honest?

With age, married or not, comes the death of loved ones. As difficult as it can be to imagine this aspect of life, people should consider and prepare for these moments as part of their retirement planning.

Couples

We develop a sense of interdependence with those close to us. We share decisions and responsibilities, and our identity is strongly and inevitably intertwined. For many, marriage and family life offer a source of love, security, emotional support and companionship.

The prospect of becoming widowed, of ending your shared experience with your spouse, is almost beyond thought. Still, you can end up far better off by giving serious thought to that eventuality. As a couple, plan for married and single life.

There are other things to be prepared for too, like an unexpected early retirement, the reality of spending far more time with your spouse than you did before retirement and whether your retirement income planning was accurate for your true expenses.

Manage Finances Together

As couples plan for retirement, the goal should be to leave each partner in a financially sound position in case something happens—like disability or death—to one of them.

Getting a handle on your entire financial position can be difficult if you leave financial matters entirely to one partner.

Too often, one partner assumes responsibility for handling bank accounts, bill payments, debts, investments and other money matters. This may create major problems—and possibly extra financial costs—should something happen to that partner.

The best way to be prepared is for those in a relationship and/or with kids to have knowledge of family affairs and experience in handling day-to-day financial matters in case they need to handle the chores alone. Spouses should work together to prepare and maintain a careful inventory of family assets. **(See the worksheets in Chapter 2.)**

Shared handling of financial matters will make lone decisions easier if a partner gets sick or dies. While this will not ease the grief, it can reduce confusion and unnecessary strain at a very trying time.

Will You Each Be Secure?

This is another question couples should think about together. Married couples' retirement planning decisions should include the goal of leaving each partner in a financially sound position.

- Is each partner's life insurance adequate? It's a good idea to review the amount of coverage you have in light of the rising cost of living. Coverage that might have been adequate when policies were taken out might be inadequate now.
- If a spouse is retired, would his or her pension terminate upon death?
- If a spouse is still working, would a pension program provide for a widow or widower if death occurs before retirement?
- Does each partner accrue his or her own retirement assets?
- What help would Social Security be? **(See more on Social Security survivor benefits in Chapter 3.)**
- Have you checked the listed beneficiary of individual retirement accounts (IRAs), 401(k)s, stock investment plans, insurance and other savings plans that either spouse may have?

Make sure you keep copies of your beneficiary forms in a safe place, along with your other estate documents.

- How about health insurance? You should check on what would happen to your partner's health insurance coverage, particularly under group insurance programs. If there are any provisions for extending coverage after an active employee or retiree dies, explore the possibilities.

Your Pension and Your Spouse

Many workers who have pension plans do not know enough about them. Many only vaguely know what they can expect in monthly payments after retirement. They have not read, or have forgotten, the fine print in pension material furnished by employers. There is an important decision that people with pensions must make before they retire: the option of pension payment.

The law requires a married employee's spouse to have an active role in deciding how the employee's pension benefits are to be paid.

Pension plans must provide a joint and survivor pension option to protect the surviving spouse of a retiree. Before a married person retires, both spouses will have to decide whether to take the joint and survivor option or choose a different form of pension. Unless a married person elects to take another form of pension, a joint and survivor pension is automatically given to the retiree.

For a defined benefit pension plan (see page 17 for description), the law requires a spouse to give written permission before an employee can choose a plan that would stop payments upon the employee's death instead of continuing payments to the surviving spouse. In other words, it is required by law that a spouse must agree to the rejection of the joint and survivor option.

Note: The requirement of spousal consent does not apply in most instances to other savings, investments and retirement accounts such as IRAs, 401(k)s, insurance and stock participation plans. Check the details of your plans.

Lifetime Benefit Pension

One form of pension is a monthly benefit for the lifetime of the retiree. The payments end when the retiree dies. Some plans may also have the option of a single lump-sum payment at retirement for you to invest and figure out for yourself how to turn that amount into a retirement paycheck for the rest of your life.

If the retiring spouse opts for the lifetime benefit pension or the single lump-sum payment, both eliminate any widow/er's benefit payments.

The retiree must have the spouse's consent and a signed spousal consent form to select these options. The form will list options for you and your spouse to consider. Do not assume that both spouses understand the choices or the spousal consent form. Also, some couples are not aware that women statistically are likely to outlive men.

The lifetime benefit pension usually provides the highest monthly benefit, so people are tempted to select it. But it will pay only while the retired spouse is alive and will end upon his or her death.

The last chance to make sure a spouse receives a survivor's pension is at the time of retirement.

Joint and Survivor Pension

The joint and survivor pension, which under the law must be offered to a married person before he or she retires, provides payments to the surviving spouse if the retiree dies first. You can think of this as benefit payments for two lifetimes if the retiree dies first. While the retiree is living and receiving pension payments, those payments will be reduced compared with a lifetime benefit pension. If the retiree dies first, then the spouse will receive some percentage of the retiree's payment for the rest of his or her life. Pension plans have varying percentages of the retiree's benefit that will be paid to a surviving spouse. How does it work?

Let's take the example of a lifetime benefit pension of $1,600 per month. If the retiree elects the 50% joint and survivor pension, the pension plan calculates a reduction considering the ages of both spouses at retirement. As an example, let's use a 12% reduction. In this case, the retiree's pension would be reduced to $1,408 a month ($1,600 x 88%). If the retiree dies first, the spouse will receive 50% of the pension payment until death. Fifty percent of $1,408 is $704 a month. If the spouse dies first, the entire reduced monthly payment ($1,408) continues until the death of the retiree. Without the 50% option, the lifetime benefit pension would be $1,600 a month while the retiree is alive, but the surviving spouse would receive zero after the retiree's death.

Deciding on a Pension Option

The decision may feel challenging because there are many unknowns. You do not know when you and your spouse will die. Who will die first? How many years between the deaths? It is a gamble because the spouse could die before the retiree. On the other hand, the spouse could live much longer than the retiree. Or you could die at the same time. Following are some steps to consider as you move through the decision-making process.

1. The first step is to gather the facts and information available to you. Find out from your pension department what the deadline is to notify them of the decision. Then you know how much time you have to gather facts and make a decision. Possible questions to ask include:
   - Will my spouse need my partial pension payments if I die? Do I have enough investments or life insurance to provide financial security without the pension after my death?
   - Does my spouse have his or her own retirement income such as Social Security, pension and/or personal retirement savings?
   - How much will my regular pension be reduced if I take the joint and survivor option? How do the two options look as part of our retirement income and expenses in the big picture?

- Does my pension plan have other payout options? What are the types and values of each payout option?
- Are there health conditions for my spouse or me that could affect our life expectancies?
- At what ages did our parents die, and what were their health histories?
- Do I have a divorce settlement from a previous marriage that affects the pension rights of my spouse?

2. Analyze the information you gathered.
3. List the advantages and disadvantages of each option.
4. Seek advice.
5. Decide.
6. Stop thinking about the decision. Don't try to second-guess yourself.

There are at least a couple of situations where the joint and survivor option is generally better:

- For a survivor who expects to depend on a spouse's pension as a source of income in retirement
- If the retiree worked for a federal, state or local government that does not require the payment of Social Security taxes. Unless you have your own Social Security and pension benefits, the joint and survivor benefit is all you would be entitled to, with the possible exception of Supplemental Security Income (SSI). **(See Chapter 3.)**

One's Retired, One's Not

Many people find themselves in retirement much earlier than anticipated. For people in relationships, their partners may continue to work. This creates a new dynamic in the home and in the relationship that can make for difficult adjustments. If married, you should plan your retirement together and take the time to develop realistic expectations about your retirement.

There is a need for planning, financial and otherwise, but many couples make the transition successfully. They approach their new circumstances—even if retirement came earlier than expected—as an opportunity to start a new career or pursue long-held plans.

Both Are Retired

Be prepared for possible challenges in your relationship. Every relationship is unique. Some couples are used to seeing each other only outside of working hours and then, after retirement, they see each other nonstop. Here are a few common sources of conflict in relationships during retirement.

- How the burden is shared when it comes to household responsibilities
- How to spend time together and apart. Even the best-laid plans, once you are actually living out those plans, may not be realistic. Based on

LIFE EXPECTANCIES

Age	Male Expectancy	Years	Female Expectancy	Years
50	79.69	29.69	83.26	33.26
55	80.52	25.52	83.85	28.85
60	81.61	21.61	84.60	24.60
65	82.92	17.92	85.49	20.49
70	84.40	14.40	86.57	16.57
75	86.18	11.18	87.97	12.97

Social Security Actuarial Life Table

The Centers for Disease Control and Prevention attributes longevity to new and better medicines, healthier lifestyles and lower reported mortality rates.

your new experiences, you may want to change your expectations and plans.

- How to spend money and reduce expenses
- How to transition from work life to home life. For example, someone whose career involved supervising people may apply those skills to managing you and the home, which could lead to friction.
- Annoying behaviors seem more amplified and intolerable.

Some solutions:

- Communicate. Openly share and actively listen.
- Be willing to share roles that have long been (or have not been) your responsibility.
- Set boundaries.
- Be willing to modify behaviors.

Plan for Loss of Spouse

Being prepared is not an indication that you are preparing for the imminent death of your partner. The chances are that you both have many happy years ahead of you. But if an accidental death or fatal illness should occur, you will be in a better position to carry on with and manage your life if you have done some preplanning. When you plan and prepare with your spouse as you always have, you can plan more securely and easily than if you are alone and under the stress and emotional upheaval of losing a loved one.

Some questions to consider are:

- How many years can I expect to live with my spouse after retirement?
- How many years will I likely live alone?
- What is my life expectancy?

Reacting to Loss of Spouse

It may not be possible to fully prepare for the shock of learning that your spouse is dying or has died. There are a wide range of reactions from the physical to the emotional, cognitive, spiritual and behavioral. But one thing you can do is try to understand the emotions you are feeling and

WIDOWHOOD RESOURCES AND SUPPORT

- Hope for Widows Foundation is a national support system for, and developed by, widowed women. www.hopeforwidows.org

- National Widowers' Organization for men www.nationalwidowers.org

- Camp Widow is a program of Soaring Spirits International created by widowed people for widowed people. This organization welcomes anyone who has outlived the person with whom they'd planned to spend the rest of their life: married, never married, planning to be married, divorced at the time of death, people of all sexes and genders, straight, LGBTQ, religious, not religious, widowed folks with kids and without kids, and complicated or conventional relationships. www.campwidow.org

realize that it is good to grieve. Grief is a natural process, a way our minds become reconciled to losing a loved one. Grief is not easily categorized into a step-by-step process. Grief is different for everyone.

You may feel guilt for not having done certain things when your spouse was alive. You may feel anger at being abandoned and left alone, at not knowing where certain things are or what needs to be done. You may feel lost without the old routines and patterns of living. You may not have anyone to eat breakfast with in the morning or talk to at night. You may be at a loss about what to do or where to go. You may feel despair, and there may be many painful days ahead, including holidays, anniversaries and birthdays. But there are resources to help. **(See "Widowhood Resources and Support" above.)**

After a Loved One's Death

The months following the death of someone you love are difficult and critical times in life. You have to deal with all kinds of emotions, without the help of someone with whom you used to share many of your worries and cares. They are critical times because you are starting, on your own, to make a new life for yourself. You will have to learn new skills, do things you never dreamed of doing and find new ways to spend your time.

No one can prevent this time in your life from being painful. But people can and will help, if you let them.

There are tasks to take care of for the deceased. Very soon, after the funeral, you may need to take care of these matters: processing the will; freeing bank accounts; changing titles on property, car, stock, etc.; settling unpaid bills; keeping accurate and complete records; applying for Social Security and funeral benefits; and filing life insurance claims.

You may need the help of an attorney or financial counselor for legal and financial matters. It will cost you some money to get help with such things, but it may cost you more in lost money if you try to do it on your own.

During the period after the death of a spouse, you may also need the emotional support that counseling can give, particularly if you find that your grieving does not lessen after about six weeks. But most of all, you need to help yourself. Find the power within yourself to start a new life and to begin to discover who you are, what your potentials are and what possibilities lie before you.

Financial Decisions to Make

Other affairs that you must take care of—but that you need not be concerned with for a while—are income taxes, budgeting, seeing that your own will is as you want it, and inheritance and estate taxes. There will be other factors if there are minor children or dependents. Keep in close communication with a knowledgeable friend or attorney to be sure all necessary tasks are accomplished.

LIFE TRANSITIONS: THINGS TO DO

When divorced, widowed or remarried:

- Change the beneficiary on investment and retirement accounts, life insurance policies and annuities.

- Update health care and financial powers of attorney, wills and living trusts.

- If property was jointly held, update the ownership status.

- Before remarrying, be aware of any legal documents from a previous marriage that are still effective.

If the spouse you lost primarily handled financial matters, you may worry about budgeting and managing money in addition to loneliness and grief. It is a good idea for spouses to plan for a potential death well in advance. Sound guidance is important at any time.

If you are inexperienced in handling finances, you could feel overwhelmed. For some, the necessity of tackling new financial tasks is therapeutic. For others, it is added strain and more unhappiness.

One of the first and toughest decisions a widow/er must make is what to do with the money from insurance policies and a partner's estate. You may suddenly have what seems to be a great deal of capital.

In regard to family savings and investment programs, proceed with care, set clear objectives based on projected annual budget needs and get expert counseling. But avoid letting capital stay idle and unproductive because of uncertainties about what should or should not be done.

Annuities can provide an assured income for life, but they limit flexibility. Once funds are committed, they cannot be retrieved or shifted.

Flexibility is necessary because of inflation, and needs may vary. It's a good idea for widow/ers to explore a variety of investment possibilities and establish a sound program that provides a basis for the use of insurance and other money.

The Impact of Divorce on Financial Planning

There are many financial planning impacts to consider following a divorce. Analyzing income and expenses is essential. Pew Research data shows that the rates of a marriage ending for people over age 50, sometimes called a *gray divorce,* have been climbing, led by Baby Boomers. The divorce rate over age 65 roughly tripled from 1990 to 2017. Gray divorcees tend to be less financially secure than married and widowed adults, particularly among women.

It can be beneficial to hire a financial planner to assist in splitting all retirement and financial accounts. A *divorce decree* is a court document that specifies the rights and responsibilities of each spouse.

In general, assets are split in some way unless both incomes and savings were equal. State law determines how assets are divided. Following are some topics to consider.

- **Beneficiaries:** After you give up or receive retirement assets, be sure to add or update beneficiaries. Some divorce decrees require an ex-spouse to remain the beneficiary.
- **Cash** in joint accounts, such as an emergency savings account, may be split or used to pay legal fees to settle the divorce.
- **Home:** Often one spouse wants to keep the house and may be willing to surrender other assets to get it. If you are keeping the home, you must determine if your individual income will cover the mortgage, taxes and upkeep. For many, it's impossible to maintain the marital standard of living in the family home on one income. You must consider if the assets you'd give up to keep the home would be better for

your long-term financial security. Check if both spouses are on the title to the home.
- **Loans:** Spouses share liability on any outstanding loans in both of your names. Refinance to remove one spouse from the loan. In community property states, in which couples are required to equally split all assets acquired during a marriage, spouses share liability on outstanding loans even in one person's name.
- **Health insurance:** If one spouse covered the couple with employer-sponsored health insurance, continuing that coverage may be an option for a limited time through a law called COBRA. This coverage can be expensive because the employer doesn't cover any portion of the ex-spouse's cost.
- **Other insurance:** You'll need insurance for the assets that become yours (e.g., car, home). You may need to get or revise life and disability insurance. Update your beneficiaries.
- **Taxes:** Taxes may be due right away for assets liquidated in the settlement. Or there may not be any tax due at divorce if assets are simply divided. But consider who will be responsible for any taxable events such as 401(k) distributions in retirement.
- **Social Security:** If you were married ten years or longer, you can receive benefits on your ex-spouse's record if that amount is higher than 100% of the benefit based on your own earnings. (**For more detail, see page 39.**)

Divorce and Retirement Savings

The rules for splitting retirement savings vary depending on the type of plan.
- **IRA:** These accounts are divided tax-free using a process known as *transfer incident to divorce.*
- **Employer-sponsored defined contribution plans:** Tax-qualified plans such as 401(k) and 403(b) plans are split under the qualified domestic relations order (QDRO) rules for a tax-free transfer of the assets to another qualified plan or IRA.

- **Defined benefit pension plans:** QDRO rules apply to splitting pensions. Legally, a court is authorized to award a spouse part of a former spouse's pension in a divorce settlement. Be careful of trading other tangible property for your rights to the pension.

A QDRO grants a person known as the *alternate payee* (the person who does not have the retirement plan) the right to part of the retirement benefits a former spouse (the *participant)* earned through an employer-sponsored retirement plan. A QDRO is separate from the divorce decree. You won't automatically get a QDRO just because your spouse has a retirement account. Make sure your divorce attorney knows your spouse has retirement savings. Often times a divorcing couple will have many retirement plans.

You need to specifically ask the court for a QDRO as part of your property settlement agreement. Ask as soon as possible because the process can take a while. The retirement plan may charge a fee to process the QDRO. The QDRO may specify which spouse pays the fee. Some plans charge a reduced fee or no fee if you use their model QDRO.

Each retirement plan has its own rules for what information needs to be included in a QDRO, and the plan administrator can accept or reject the order based upon minute details. Be sure to enter the plan name exactly.

Especially if retirement is years or decades away, it can be difficult to remember that the time to divide retirement assets is now. Having the divorce decree and QDRO issued at the same time and submitting them to the plan immediately will protect you once it comes time to distribute retirement assets.

Singles

People will age alone for many reasons. Some have led a single life; others were once part of a couple and became single due to death or divorce. If you're single, do some planning to ensure you have a support system for your financial matters and your physical and emotional health. Examples of what you might need from your support system as you age include people to:
- Let you know when it's time to stop driving
- Notice signs of decline in your abilities to do daily tasks and find appropriate help
- Pay bills and monitor bank accounts.

Additional considerations for singles include life insurance and beneficiary designations. If single people don't have a dependent who is relying on their income, then they don't need life insurance. Money saved on life insurance policies can be used to bolster retirement savings or in other important facets of their lives. For some single people, beneficiary designations are not as automatic. If there is not a partner or child, single people may want to consider options such as extended family members, close friends or charities as their beneficiary designations.

Single Parenting

If your child's other parent is responsible for paying child support, you are not alone if those payments don't arrive or arrive only sporadically. The U.S. Census Bureau reported that approximately two-thirds of custodial parents who were due child support received some payments from noncustodial parents, and only 43.5% reported receiving the full amount of child support due. It can make budgeting more challenging, but it might be safer not to count on child support payments as income for your budget. This means your own income will have to cover essentials. Use child support that does arrive for nonessentials.

No Children

As you age, there are additional considerations if you didn't have a child, have lost a child or have a child who is not available to help you as you grow older. Solo agers, who may be single or coupled with no children, may need to do some extra planning for how to stay safe, happy, connected and satisfied with their lives.

It is hard but necessary to consider what might happen to you physically and socially as you age and how you might prepare for those realities. Plan when you are still independent in case an emergency or sudden decline should occur. This also gives you time to build relationships with relatives, younger friends you meet through leisure and volunteering, and neighbors. Once you plan for what might happen, stop worrying and enjoy life.

Finding someone trustworthy to take over financial or health care decisions can be a challenge. A responsible younger friend or relative may be an option. You might consider hiring a professional fiduciary. In California and Arizona, people can hire state-licensed fiduciaries for financial and health care decisions. Other states don't have licensing, but an estate planning attorney or financial planner may be able to refer you to a reputable personal fiduciary.

The California Professional Fiduciaries Bureau was created by law to regulate non-family-member professional fiduciaries, including conservators, guardians, trustees and agents under durable power of attorney as defined by the Professional Fiduciaries Act. See **www.fiduciary.ca.gov.**

In Arizona, for a fee, the Fiduciary Licensing Program trains and certifies individuals who serve as court-appointed guardians, conservators and personal representatives. See **www.azcourts .gov/cld/Fiduciary-Licensing-Program/Public -Information.**

PLANNING TIPS FOR SOLO AGERS

Sara Zeff Geber, a retirement coach and author of *Essential Retirement Planning for Solo Agers: A Retirement and Aging Roadmap for Single and Childless Adults,* lists the responsibilities that adult children or other trusted adults may take on:

- Caregiving and supervising caregivers
- Figuring out the best housing
- Emotional support
- Practical support: e.g., driving you to appointments, running errands, chores
- Money management
- Health care or legal power of attorney
- Social connectedness.

Ask yourself: What outside assistance will I need to meet these responsibilities? Identify people who are available to occasionally check in on you and provide support for these responsibilities and anything else you might need. Your housing decision is important to your safety and social connection. See housing options in Chapter 9.

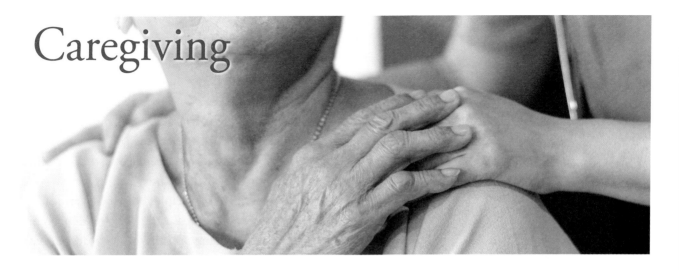

Caregiving

"There are only four kinds of people in the world: those who have been caregivers, those who are caregivers, those who will be caregivers and those who will need caregivers."

—Rosalynn Carter

Caring for Others

A caregiver can be any relative, partner, friend or neighbor who provides a broad range of assistance for people who need help to function on a daily basis. Caregivers can be young or old; there is a huge range of when people find themselves as a caregiver or, for that matter, as a care recipient. But because people are living longer, it is common for elder caregiving responsibilities to increase near or during retirement. Grandparents may provide child care for working parents or become primary caregivers for grandchildren. As longevity increases, people may find themselves as late-in-life caregivers. People age 75 can be caring for parents age 95 and older, a growing phenomenon called *aging together.* If possible, early planning with people who could potentially receive care from you—because of age, illness and/or disability—is important. Many of us don't automatically have a lot of caregiver skills. This chapter will talk about elder and other types of caregiving, what caregiving involves, and tips for caregivers to manage their own health and finances.

Rewards and Challenges

For many people, caregiving has positive associations such as feeling a sense of fulfillment, purpose and gratitude. Other benefits include new social connections and learning. While caregiving can be a rewarding experience, caregivers often face challenges. Some of the common challenges caregivers face are:

- **Time:** Caregiving duties take time away from other things like family, leisure, exercise, meal preparation and work. Social connections with friends and co-workers may become strained.
- **Lack of privacy:** When a care recipient lives with you, especially in a small space, it can be difficult to find a place to be alone.
- **Financial strain:** Unpaid caregiving comes with expenses. Some caregiving interferes with work, which can affect income and employer-sponsored benefits.
- **Sleep:** Often an elder loved one's sleep-wake cycle can be mixed up, leading to sleep deprivation for the caregiver. (**See page 80 for more information on sleep.**)

CAREGIVERS BY THE NUMBERS: CURRENT AND FUTURE

- Annually, about 26 million people, or one in ten adults, care for a parent or spouse, and about 22 million people care for other adult relatives, such as grandparents, aunts and uncles, or people not related to them, according to the U.S. Bureau of Labor Statistics (BLS).

- Women are more likely than men to provide care.

- Close to 30% of parental or spousal caregivers provide care for more than one person.

- The average age of parental caregivers is 50, and the average age of spousal caregivers is 70.

- Sixteen percent of caregivers provided care for more than ten years.

As the number of older Americans increases, so will the number of caregivers needed to provide care.

- The Centers for Disease Control and Prevention (CDC) estimates the number of people age 65 and older is expected to double between 2000 and 2030.

- There will be 71 million people age 65 and older when all Baby Boomers are at least 65 years old in 2030.

- Currently, there are seven potential family caregivers per adult. By 2030, there will be only four potential family caregivers per adult.

- **Physical stress:** Tasks that help with mobility and dressing—including lifting, pushing, pulling and bending—can be hard on the caregiver's body.

- **Emotional stress:** Caregivers report feeling a range of emotions: overwhelmed, burdened, confused, sad, anxious, guilty and intimidated by their duties. Some feel shame or fear about asking for help from others. Some feel angry when a care recipient is not cooperating. Some caregivers tell themselves that negative emotions mean they are weak or not a good caregiver. Feeling helpless or alone can lead to isolation and increase the risk for depression. Another challenge is thinking you do not have time to seek counseling.

Caregiving Starts Younger and Lasts Longer

- **Caring for grandparents:** Young caregivers may face additional challenges. They may have less life experience to call on for dealing with government agencies and the health care system. They are more likely to be getting a career or family started. Caregiving demands may result in their becoming socially isolated from people their same age. In addition, there may be challenging dynamics with parents who are unavailable for caregiving because of distance or other reasons. Solutions for young caregivers to stay on track with building a future include locating caregiving services and respite care funding. **(See page 153.)**

- **Generation X caregivers:** According to a survey by Transamerica Institute on the impact of caregiving by generation, Generation X caregivers are facing multiple financial-related challenges. Top financial priorities are paying off debt, covering basic living expenses, saving for retirement and supporting children. Generation X caregivers have saved the least for retirement, compared with other generations. About 19% of Generation X caregivers reported having nothing saved for retirement.

- **Millennial caregivers:** One in four family caregivers is a Millennial, according to an AARP Public Policy Institute report. About 73% of

Millennial caregivers are employed, but many have low incomes, with one in three having a household income of less than $30,000 a year. Millennial caregivers are almost twice as likely as older caregivers to be caring for someone with emotional or mental health issues, therefore facing a higher emotional strain. Compared with older caregivers, Millennials spend a higher percentage of their income on expenses such as home modifications for the care recipient as well as food and transportation.

Solutions

■ **Respite care:** Respite care is a service that allows caregivers to take a break from their caregiving duties so they can attend to their own needs, whether it's to focus on their own health or address other challenges listed in the previous section. In general, a primary caregiver, who takes on the greatest responsibility for daily care, needs respite care. You should consider respite care much earlier than you think you will need it. Respite care will be most helpful if you use it before you become sleep-deprived, isolated and/or overwhelmed. Respite care should be beneficial and enjoyable to the care recipient too. Respite services usually charge by the hour or by the day. Most insurance plans do not cover these costs. Some states provide funding. **Check www .archrespite.org/respitelocator for providers, programs and funding in your area.**

If an aging loved one lives with you, it can help to have them participate as much as possible in household chores and stick to a routine that includes activities to keep them active, such as sports, hobbies, family events and respite care.

■ **Geriatric care manager:** A geriatric care manager, usually a licensed nurse or social worker who specializes in geriatrics, is a sort of "professional relative" who can help caregivers figure out their needs and come up with a plan that is financially feasible. For example,

geriatric care managers can evaluate housing options (including in-home care needs), select home health care providers and help with family conflicts.

Fees vary, and most care managers charge by the hour. They can be expensive. Medicare does not pay for this service, and most insurance plans do not either. To avoid surprise costs, ask about fees, out-of-pocket expenses and billing right away, and get them in writing. If you don't understand, ask for clarification until you feel comfortable with the financial obligations. **For more information and to find a geriatric care manager, visit:**

■ **Aging Life Care Association: www .aginglifecare.org**
■ **Eldercare Locator: www.eldercare.acl.gov**
■ **National Institute on Aging: www.nia.nih .gov/health/what-geriatric-care-manager.**

Children Who Have Special Needs

Some geriatric care managers also help younger adults who have a disability (physical and developmental) or serious illness (brain injury) and their families. For example, people may have physical disabilities, developmental disabilities, (e.g., Down Syndrome, autism spectrum disorder), mental illness or brain injury. These professionals can help parents who have an adult child with disabilities come up with a plan for the current and future needs of their child.

Families With Special Needs: Caregiving Tips

Caregiving for a special needs child may mean advocating for the right special education supports at school. **For more information about individualized education programs (IEPs), including eligibility, how an IEP is developed and how to prepare for meetings, go to www .understood.org/en/school-learning/special -services/ieps.**

As a special needs child becomes an adult, there are additional considerations for individuals and families alike. **For more information and tips on getting support, being an advocate and taking care of yourself, visit the Centers for Disease Control and Prevention web page at www.cdc .gov/family/specialneeds/index.htm.**

See page 57 for estate planning considerations that may ensure a child is taken care of past your lifetime.

Aging Parent or Grandparent

As you plan for yourself in retirement, you may also need to plan with your parent(s). Having open and honest conversations with your loved ones about caregiving preferences at an early stage, before emergencies like a fall, accident or diagnosis, is ideal. If possible, discuss and coordinate with all family members. Talking about money is uncomfortable for many people, but it is essential to caregiving planning because finances will guide decisions once a parent needs care. Prepare for family challenges like emotions, differing opinions and varying contributions. It may not be easy to tackle the touchy subjects of aging and sickness. But whether you talk on the phone or in person, it's vital that you understand what your parents want and need and how you can help. Preparing now can give you and your parents the peace of mind that comes from knowing that the family will be able to provide the help they may need.

- Reread Chapter 5 on estate planning. Instead of reading it with yourself in mind, view it as applying to your parent to get an idea of the information you need to seek.
- Take inventory. Both you and your parents should know what assets exist. Learn where to find the paperwork on brokerage accounts, investments and pensions as well as legal documents such as titles and wills. Talk about which assets or insurance can be tapped for assisted living or nursing home care (e.g., home equity, cash value life insurance, long-term care insurance).

- There are some steps you can take while your parents are healthy and active to ensure that, no matter how far apart you live, you'll be prepared in an emergency.
- Establish a communications network. Meet the people in your parents' lives—friends, neighbors, doctors, financial advisor—and exchange contact information. Make sure you know who has keys to the home. Be sure to have a procedure in place in case of an emergency.
- Keep a current list of local ambulance services, hospitals, doctors, medications and medical conditions.
- Be sure your parents have a durable power of attorney, which gives someone they choose the authority to handle their financial affairs. Establish a durable power of attorney for health care or health care proxy; and draft a living will, spelling out their wishes regarding life support. **(See more about advance directives on page 58.)**
- Once you become a caretaker for your parents, continue to involve them in your family by discussing all plans and decisions. Make them a part of the process.

Resources for Talking and Planning

- AARP *Prepare to Care Guide* on how to start a conversation (with checklist): **www.aarp.org/ caregiving/prepare-to-care-planning-guide**
- Eldercare Locator fact sheets address issues faced by older adults and family caregivers: **https://eldercare.acl.gov/Public/Resources /Factsheets/Index.aspx.** For example, the fact sheet "Face the Facts" explains important topics to discuss with parents and suggests questions to ask to get the conversation going about finances, health care, personal care and legal matters.

What Caregivers Do

Caregivers are responsible for many tasks and decisions. The following list is just a few.

- Deciding on housing and/or where to live
- Tracking behavior and cognitive impairment
- Figuring out what is needed and when
- Providing transportation to medical appointments
- Scheduling medical appointments. Caregivers with proxy access to the hospital system online patient portal can use this as a central place to view test results, contact doctors, make appointments and pay bills.
- Picking up prescription drugs and/or managing refills with an online or mail-order pharmacy.
- Determining eligibility and filling out applications for benefits and services.
  - The National Council on Aging (NCOA) program has an online "BenefitsCheckUp" program that finds programs for seniors that may pay for some of their prescription drugs, health care, food, clothing, housing, utilities, and other essential items or services. There are also home repair programs that can help you fix safety issues found in your home. **Check www.benefitscheckup.org.** Have records about income, assets and expenses available before you get started.
- Helping with end-of-life care

LGBTQIA+ Community

The language used to talk about people with various sexual and gender identities is always evolving and can mean different things to different people. With inclusivity in mind, the older acronym, LGBT, has been expanded to LGBTQIA+, which stands for lesbian, gay, bisexual, transgender, queer and/or questioning, intersex, and asexual and/or ally. A plus sign is meant to cover anyone else who is not described by those words. As you will see in the following resources, the research and surveying of older adults so far tends to use the LGBT acronym.

- By 2030, there will be an estimated seven million LGBT people in America over the age of 50. About 4.7 million of them will need elder care and related services, according to Advocacy

FINANCIAL SUPPORT

According to a Merrill Lynch and Age Wave study of people age 50 and over, family members are increasingly turning to each other for a financial helping hand.

- Six in ten people provided financial support to adult children, grandchildren, parents and/or siblings during the last five years.
- The vast majority of people have never budgeted or prepared for providing financial support to other family members (88%) or caring for an aging parent or relative (91%) even though they are likely to provide such support.
- The amount of help provided can be substantial. The average support for family members in the last five years totaled $14,900.

Balance your family needs with your own retirement financial security. Be honest with your family and yourself about how much you can give. Giving too much without accounting for your own future needs may require you to be relying on family support in retirement.

Sixty percent of caregivers are women, according to data from the Women's Institute for a Secure Retirement (WISER). Women are more likely to interrupt their careers or retire early for caregiving. WISER data also shows:

- On average, women caregivers lose $324,000 in lost wages, Social Security benefits and retirement plans over a lifetime.
- Women caregivers are more likely than noncaregivers to end up in poverty.

and Services for LGBT Elders (SAGE). Three-quarters of LGBT people are worried about having adequate family or social supports, according to AARP research.

- *Facts of LGBT Aging:* **www.sageusa.org/wp-content/uploads/2018/05/sageusa-the-facts-on-lgbt-aging.pdf**
- *Maintaining Dignity: Understanding and Responding to the Challenges Facing Older LGBT Americans:* **www.aarp.org/research/topics/life/info-2018/maintaining-dignity-lgbt.html**
- *Prepare to Care: A Planning Guide for Caregivers in the LGBT Community:* **www.aarp.org/content/dam/aarp/home-and-family/caregiving/2017/05/prepare-to-care-guide-lgbt-aarp.pdf**
- *A Guide to LGBT Caregiving:* **www.nextstepincare.org/uploads/File/Guides/LGBT/LGBT_Guide.pdf**

Caring for a Person Aging at Home

As more people are reaching old age, there is an increase in the number of people receiving home health care through agencies or private arrangements. Most people would prefer to stay in their own home instead of moving to a nursing home. Aging in place is also less expensive. But there are safety issues to watch out for. See page 116 for a safety checklist.

Caregivers have added responsibilities of managing a home. Checking the fridge is a regular task. Be aware of behaviors like stockpiling and storing things in the fridge that don't belong there, which can be early signs of dementia. Throw out food that might not be safe. A food-related illness can be life-threatening for an older person. Get a sense for the nutritional needs of a loved one and whether those needs are being met.

This is a short list of what else a caregiver may need to do in the home.

- Feed and clean up after pets
- Perform or arrange for maintenance and repairs
- Follow the garbage and recycling schedule

- Organize medications weekly
- Install a medical alert system
- Monitor physical and emotional symptoms
- Arrange visitors and social outings
- Order adaptive devices and teach how to use them
- Teach how to use technology (e.g., mobile phone, tablet)
- Hire and supervise in-home help
- Figure out payments for home health care services. Note: Medicare Parts A and B pay for medically necessary intermittent visits for skilled nursing or physical therapy.

What are you as a caregiver going to be able to do yourself or with the help of other family? Do you need to hire help for anything?

Hiring In-Home Help

A fact sheet by Family Caregiver Alliance explains how to find home care agencies or private hires. Visit www.caregiver.org/hiring-home-help.

A word-of-mouth referral is one approach to finding a caregiver for hire. Check with people in your parents' social circles. Someone might be able to recommend a person who can help. Ask doctors for referrals.

Visit these sources to search for home health care in your area.

- Medicare Home Health Compare lists home health agencies: **www.medicare.gov/homehealthcompare/search.html**
- National Association of Home Care and Hospice Location Service: **https://agencylocator.nahc.org**

Supervising In-Home Help

Similar to any person you hire to do a job, it's important to carefully screen the candidates before hiring a caregiver and to follow up after hiring to monitor the job the caregiver is doing. As a rule, no caregiver—unless bonded—should deal with a care recipient's finances. The power of attorney should handle finances.

Long-Distance Caregiving

If you don't live in the vicinity of the person who needs care (say, an hour or more away), you can still be involved in planning and caregiving. Or, if you live close by but siblings live at a distance, here are some ideas of what they can do to help out. Long-distance caregiving can take many forms. The following are just a few.

- Managing finances
- Setting up automatic bill pay
- Searching for elder care services and making calls
- Researching health conditions, medications and provider credentials
- Finding and organizing information, and keeping it updated
- Managing insurance benefits and claims
- Providing respite care for a primary caregiver
- Planning for emergencies
- Providing updates to family and friends

Review the list of what caregivers do on pages 154-155 to see if any of those tasks can be done from a distance. The caregiving you can provide is an individualized decision, and your tasks may change over time.

For more ways you can support from afar, go to www.nia.nih.gov/health/caregiving/long -distance-caregiving.

Not sure what to do? Below are some ways for new long-distance caregivers to get started.

- Ask the primary caregiver, if there is one, and the care recipient how you can help.
- Talk to friends who have caregiving experience to see if they have suggestions.
- Find out more about local resources that might be useful.
- Develop a good understanding of the person's health issues and other needs.
- Visit when you can. You might notice something that needs to be done and that can be taken care of from a distance.

Choosing an Assisted Living Home

If home care is not an option and a parent or spouse is still in good health but needs support with eating, bathing, dressing, moving around or managing medication, assisted living may provide a feeling of independence. Before picking a facility, check out the range and quality of services that are provided, such as social activities, transportation and access to medical assistance. If the facility provides meals, review the menus and be sure to taste a few meals.

Choosing a Nursing Home

If a parent or spouse is unable to live alone, requires supervision, is chronically ill and/or needs help with daily activities that go beyond the scope of home care, a nursing home may be needed. Choosing a nursing home is an emotional, medical and financial decision. Approximately one-half of all nursing home admissions come directly after hospital stays; a patient can have as little as one day to pick a nursing home. Planning will make an informed decision easier. Other common reasons for nursing home placement are incontinence, risk to caregiver of self-injury from heavy lifting, and anger on the part of the caregiver or care recipient.

Before picking a nursing home, you must do your homework. Ask for recommendations from friends and doctors. Involve your parent or spouse in the decision. Visit potential nursing homes with and without an appointment to view how the staff and residents interact with each other. When you revisit a nursing home, go on different days and times. Make multiple visits before you make your final decision. Talk with residents, their families and staff for their opinions and experiences. And taste the food. Review what services the home will provide, including social, recreational, spiritual or cultural. Ask if they have multiple options for living spaces, if there is a waiting list and if there is adequate security. Get the fee schedule for room, meals and other services in writing. Read the nursing home agreement carefully before signing. If possible, the resident should sign the agreement. If this is not possible and you have to sign the agreement, only sign as the resident's agent. This way you will not be personally responsible for payments.

CAREGIVERS WHO WORK

According to data from the National Alliance for Caregiving, 68% of working parental and spousal caregivers experienced job impacts. Job impacts include:

- Quitting or cutting back hours from full-time to part-time

- Going in late, leaving early or taking time off during the day

- Taking a leave of absence

- Retiring early

- Turning down a promotion.

The Government Accountability Office (GAO) studied the retirement security risks that parental and spousal caregivers face and found that, because of job impacts, caregivers may not be eligible for employer-sponsored retirement programs and may lose eligibility or vesting rights to employer contributions. Paying for caregiving expenses can also impact the ability to save.

You may be entitled to unpaid job-protected leave in a 12-month period through the Family and Medical Leave Act (FMLA). Some states have paid family leave laws. Ask if your employer offers any programs or benefits to help caregivers. More employers are offering flexible work arrangements including flexible hours, telecommuting, compressed workweeks and other options that can make it easier for caregivers to balance responsibilities. Many employers offer an employee assistance program (EAP) that can refer you to long-term care service providers and to counseling services and support groups for caregivers.

Before leaving a job or switching to part-time work, the Women's Institute for a Secure Retirement (WISER) recommends caregivers exhaust all other options. Questions to ask yourself include:

- Are you fully vested in your retirement benefit?

- Are you near an employment milestone that will get you a higher retirement benefit?

- Will you lose employer health insurance?

- Are you on track with debt reduction and other financial goals?

- What will your new budget look like with added caregiving expenses? **(See page 10 on budgeting.)**

To compare nursing homes, go to www.medicare.gov /nursinghomecompare/search .html.

To read a guide for choosing a nursing home (with a checklist), go to www .nia.nih.gov/health/choosing -nursing-home.

Paying for Long-Term Care

It is common to misunderstand which federal government programs pay for long-term care services. The resident will have to pay for long-term care services that are not covered by a public program or private insurance. Long-term care covers a range of services and support for personal care needs.

Medicare only pays for skilled services or rehabilitative care for a short period of time. Most long-term care isn't medical care. Instead, it is help with basic personal tasks of everyday life, sometimes called *activities of daily living.*

Medicaid pays for the largest share of long-term care services. To be eligible for Medicaid, you must have limited income and assets. Most assets must be depleted or transferred at least five years before a resident enters a nursing home. **See www.longtermcare. gov for Medicaid long-term care services and financial eligibility information.** Each state has its own rules regarding income and asset limits. There are also functional requirements for activities of daily living. Under Medicaid, states generally must provide institutional care to Medicaid beneficiaries, while home- and community-based long-term care services are generally an optional service.

Some of these programs include self-directed services under which Medicaid beneficiaries can hire certain relatives to provide personal care service. The program details vary greatly. Contact your state department of health services to find out more.

Financial Elder Abuse

Elder abuse doesn't always mean physical harm. Many seniors become victims of financial abuse. In its financial form, abuse is the exploitation of people to gain access to their property, investments, cash or real estate. Scams include identity theft, telemarketing, pressure to sign something we do not understand or an empty promise to provide care in exchange for property. The abuser can be a caregiver, relative, financial professional or stranger.

Not only are older people heavily targeted by scammers, but brain science and psychological data suggest that, as we get older, we become more vulnerable to fraud because our ability to detect sketchy situations may decline. We may become prone to seeing the upside of a risky deal and blowing off the downside. Some people are more inclined to believe the last person they spoke to. Others may lose the ability to push back against a high-pressure scammer. Researchers say that this vulnerability goes beyond changes in the brain. "It also involves all of these other social and environmental factors like social isolation, cultural and societal factors, and older adults having more wealth compared with younger generations," said Marti DeLiema, a research scholar at the Stanford Center on Longevity. Data from Peter Lichtenberg, Ph.D., a psychologist who studies the capacity for financial decision-making at Wayne State, shows that 20% of older people admit that they talk with others about money out of loneliness. Older people might talk to a scammer simply because they want

to talk to someone. Experts suggest the best way to help elderly people avoid financial abuse is to be present in their lives. Build up the social support system of your vulnerable loved ones.

Find tips to avoid financial fraud in Chapters 6 and 9.

For more information on elder financial abuse, go to:
- **MarketPlace Brains and Losses series: www .marketplace.org/collection/brains-losses -aging-financial-vulnerability**
- **The National Center on Elder Abuse (NCEA): https://.ncea.acl.gov**
- **American Bar Association: Protecting the Elderly from Financial Abuse: www.aba.com /consumers/pages/protectingtheelderly.aspx.**

Caring for Veterans

Veterans enrolled in Veterans Affairs (VA) health care may apply for VA long-term care services. Services at home and in the community are part of the VA medical benefits package and may be prioritized based on VA service-connected disability. All veterans enrolled in the VA medical benefits package are eligible for the following services.
- Geriatric evaluation to assess care needs and to create a care plan
- Adult day health care
- Respite care
- Skilled home health care

Residential settings and nursing homes each have different eligibility requirements. The VA does not pay for room and board in residential settings such as assisted living or adult family homes.

For information on long-term care, visit www.va.gov/geriatrics. For more on caregiver support, visit www.caregiver.va.gov.

Grandparenting

Grandparenting can provide a sense of continuity and stability throughout the years, both for you and your grandchild. It is a way for you to keep feeling vital and important and to make a contribution that is meaningful for all concerned. It can be a pure form of love and affection, providing you with companionship, pleasure and pride.

Spending on Grandkids

Grandparenting can be both a joy and a financial responsibility. According to an AARP study, the projected annual spend by grandparents on their grandchildren is $179 billion per year, which represents an average of $2,562 per grandparent per year. Grandparents are helping with education, day-to-day expenses such as meals and groceries, and vacations. Some grandparents pay major expenses such as rent or mortgage payments and medical costs.

Long-Distance Grandparenting

Distance and busy schedules are the biggest barriers to seeing grandchildren. You may be concerned that you live too far from your grandchildren to be an active grandparent. One solution is to embrace technology such as video chat and text to stay connected with grandchildren. Another possibility for grandparents who want to spend concentrated quality time with their grandchildren is to invite them for an extended stay. Also consider trips that are just for grandparents and grandchildren, so-called *skip-gen travel*. When traveling with your grandchild, be sure to take a notarized letter—signed by both parents—stating that you have permission to travel with the child and to make medical decisions for the child.

Providing Regular Care to Grandchildren

As child-care costs continue to rise, more and more grandparents are stepping in to care for infants and toddlers, filling a major gap in access to affordable, quality child care. Grandparents care for one out of four children under the age of five. These grandparents are a major influence on young lives.

Half of grandparents reported at least some conflict with adult children over issues like discipline, meals and screen time for grandchildren, according to a Zero to Three survey. It helps to talk through expectations with parents about child-rearing, scheduling, communicating about care, and managing conflict before the child-care arrangement begins and on an ongoing basis.

For grandparent caregiver resources, to go www.zerotothree.org/grandparents.

Raising Grandchildren

Perhaps your concern is not that you don't see your grandchildren enough but rather that you see them more than you had originally bargained for. Being a primary caregiver to grandchildren is not an uncommon circumstance and, for some, it can be very trying. There are many reasons for taking in grandchildren or children of other relatives. For some caregivers, the situation is temporary, when a parent is unavailable due to illness or military service. Transitions that come with divorce or long-distance moves may lead to short time periods when you become a primary caregiver. For others, the reasons are sadder and harder: the early death of parents, long-term illness, incarceration, homelessness, teen pregnancy or child neglect. Another sad reason is the growing impact of opioid use disorder and other parental substance abuse.

There is increasing awareness that placing children with relatives when they cannot remain with their parents can reduce the trauma of separation and result in better outcomes for children than placement with nonrelatives. The value of your commitment to your grandchildren should not be underestimated. It may be hard work, but your efforts can live on in the resilience of your grandchildren.

Challenges

Much depends on the reason for parental separation and the age of the children. Some of the challenges of raising grandchildren include:

- **Your own mixed feelings:** However much you love your grandchildren, taking them into your home and caring for them is a big change. Most grandparents feel a combination of resentment, love, anger and sadness about their own child and gratitude that they can provide for the grandchildren.
- **The grandchildren's feelings:** Whatever the reason, separation from a parent is a loss.
- **Relationship with your child:** Many things put a strain on this relationship. There may be times of conflict over how to raise the children. There may be times when you are torn between supporting your child and doing what is in the best interests of grandchildren.
- **Relationship with the grandchildren:** There is a big difference between being the visiting grandparent who can spoil a child or bend the rules and being a daily nurturer and disciplinarian. This change is emotional for you and the grandchild.
- **Your health:** Your health and well-being are critical to the health and well-being of your grandchildren. While the opportunity to raise a grandchild may offer a second chance at parenting for some, the challenges and unexpected demands of raising a grandchild may also result in stress-related illnesses such as high blood pressure and depression. Do what you can to stay healthy, active and relaxed. (**See Chapter 7 for ideas.**)
- **Legal issues:** Legal guardians have the same rights as a parent. Without legal guardianship, you might not be able to make medical decisions or gain access to education records.
- **Social Security:** Social Security will pay benefits to grandchildren when a grandparent retires, becomes disabled or dies, if certain conditions are met. In general, the biological parents of the child must be deceased or disabled, or the grandparent must legally adopt the grandchild. There are more criteria to receive a benefit.
- **Social isolation:** Time that you used to dedicate to your friends or your spouse may not fit into a new schedule that is focused on grandchildren.
- **Finances:** If you are working, this type of caregiving may interrupt your career. If you are retired, your standard of living may be impacted by the expenses of raising grandchildren.

Solutions

You are not alone. Whether raising grandchildren is a result of choice or obligation, there are plenty of others just like you, and support is available. Children and caregivers can benefit from services such as support groups and mental health counseling. Kinship navigator programs can support caregivers with legal assistance, referrals to child care, eligibility for benefits, respite care and much more.

Creating friendships with parents of similarly aged children may take time but is a great way to build up your local support system. Even if you come from a different generation, you will have common experiences to share with each other.

Resources for Raising Grandchildren

To connect with others and search a database of state laws and legal topic areas directly impacting these types of families, **go to www.grandfamilies .org.**

"GrandFacts" for grandfamilies include state-specific data and programs as well as information about public benefits, educational assistance, legal relationship options and state laws. **Find your state at www.grandfamilies.org/State-Fact-Sheets.**

Finding Help With Caregiving

Elder Care

- To find state offices on aging, click on "Resources Near You" at www.hhs.gov/aging.

- At www.eldercare.acl.gov, the Eldercare Locator can help you find area agencies on aging or disability resource centers, community-based organizations and geriatric care managers. Eldercare Locator can point caregivers in the right direction for training and services like meals, home care, transportation or respite care.

- Transitions between care settings (e.g., hospital to home, start of home care agency services) are often rushed, so miscommunication and errors can occur. "Next Step in Care" provides information to help family caregivers and health care providers work together to plan and implement safe and smooth transitions for chronically or seriously ill patients. Visit www.nextstepincare.org and www.nextstepincare.org/Caregiver_Home.

- Health in Aging Foundation: www.healthinaging.org

Educating Yourself About Caregiving

- Caring for your spouse: www.wellspouse.org

- Caring for people with disabilities: www.easterseals.com and www.cdc.gov/ncbddd /disabilityandhealth/family.html

- Rosalynn Carter Institute for Caregiving: www.rosalynncarter.org

- Caregiver Action Network: www.caregiveraction.org

- Family Caregiver Alliance: www.caregiver.org/caregiving

- Specific caregiving issues and strategies: www.caregiver.org/fact-sheets

- Caregiving: A Public Health Priority: www.cdc.gov/aging/caregiving

- Managing someone else's money for financial caregivers: www.consumerfinance.gov/consumer-tools /managing-someone-elses-money

Opioid Use Disorder

- The Substance Abuse and Mental Health Services Administration has resources for understanding addiction, finding treatment and paying for it at www.findtreatment.gov.

- Advocates for Opioid Recovery: www.opioidrecovery.org

- National Institute on Drug Abuse: www.drugabuse.gov/patients-families

Specific Conditions

Many associations support people with specific conditions and their caregivers.

- American Association of People with Disabilities: www.aapd.org

- American Cancer Society: www.cancer.org

- American Parkinson's Disease Association: www.apdaparkinson.org

- Attention Deficit Disorder Association: www.add.org

- Autism Spectrum Disorder: www.autismspeaks.org

- Center for Disability Rights: www.cdrnys.org

- Children and Adults with Attention Deficit/ Hyperactivity Disorder: www.chadd.org

- National Alliance on Mental Illness: www.nami.org

Alzheimer's Disease

The Alzheimer's Association reports that one in three seniors dies with Alzheimer's or another dementia. It is the sixth-leading cause of death overall in the United States, but estimates indicate that Alzheimer's may rank third—just behind heart disease and cancer—as a cause of death for older people. Currently, about six million people are living with Alzheimer's, and more than 16 million people provide unpaid care for them. By 2050, the number of people with Alzheimer's dementia is expected to rise to nearly 14 million if there are no medical breakthroughs to prevent, slow or cure the disease.

Who are the caregivers for people with Alzheimer's or other dementia?

- About one in three caregivers is age 65 or older.

- Two-thirds of caregivers are women. More specifically, over one-third of dementia caregivers are daughters.

- One-quarter of dementia caregivers are from the sandwich generation, meaning that they care for an aging parent as well as children under age 18.

- Compared with caregivers of people without dementia, twice as many caregivers of those with dementia indicate substantial emotional, financial and physical difficulties.

Finding Help With Alzheimer's Caregiving

- To find local Alzheimer's Association chapters, programs and support groups, visit www.alz.org /help-support/caregiving

- Learn more about Alzheimer's disease at www.nia.nih.gov/health/alzheimers-disease-fact -sheet.

- Learn how you can become an effective caregiver at www.nia.nih.gov/health/alzheimers /caregiving.